"An honest telling of her journey toward surrender, Teresa Swanstrom Anderson is a friend we can relate to. From childhood to motherhood she recounts the lessons that have shaped her into the woman she is today. For the woman looking for kinship and inspiration, she will find both in this book."

—**Alexandra Kuykendall,**
Author of *Loving My Actual Life,*
Co-host of "The Open Door Sisterhood" podcast

"Faith is the evidence of things not seen, and you will find in this book a life lived believing over and over again in the not yet visible plans of God. Teresa's journey to believe in the impossible will encourage you to do the same."

—**Jessica Honegger,**
Founder of Noonday Collection

"Teresa is one of the most beautiful people I've encountered in a long time. She has a soul that is genuine and invites people into her life with open arms. Her book feels exactly like she makes people feel: included and part of a greater story that is happening. And she's determined to help people find hope. Her story is life-giving and life-changing. After reading her words, I knew there was an interruption God nudged in my heart that needed revisiting. This is a great message!"

—**Nicki Koziarz,**
Author & Speaker for Proverbs 31 Ministries

"If you want to travel roads you've never been, you need a new road map. Through her own compelling story, Teresa leads us on an adventure away from the safe, me-centered life, and toward a destination that holds the richer treasures of trust, wholeness, and surrender. Her story compels us to courageously change our own."

—**Krista Gilbert,**
Author of *Reclaiming Home,* Cofounder of The Open Door Sisterhood,
Co-host of "The Open Door Sisterhood" podcast

"This is more than a book. It's an adventure. In the following pages you are invited to join an incredible adventure through the story of one family. You will undoubtedly discover what God can do if you allow your life to be beautifully interrupted."

—Nirup Alphonse,
Lead Pastor at LIFEGATE Denver

"With the voice, vulnerability, and comfortable humor of your best friend, Teresa invites you to see the often uncomfortable call of following Jesus as an opportunity to be refined, renewed, and beautified in the mess. Her entertaining, yet gospel-centered writing style is a breath of fresh air in a culture that sometimes waters down Christianity to a more comfortable, me-centered life. Teresa's words and stories will bring comfort, laughter, and hope as she shares how God interrupted the life she thought she wanted, and instead brought her to an incredibly beautiful life that's more than she ever dreamed. This is one book I will definitely be buying for all of my friends."

—Karen Stott,
Founder of Intentional Home, author of *An Intentional Life*

"I am inspired by Teresa's bold faith and her deep and wide perspective on the world. So many of us hear about distant lands crying out for help, but Teresa heard those cries, and actually did something about it. She discovered her purpose on this earth and welcomed children into her home from across the globe. No matter your story or journey, *Beautifully Interrupted* will challenge you to ask the big question: am I serving the purpose that God has for me on this earth?"

—Megan Alexander,
Author of *Faith in The Spotlight*,
TV Host on *Inside Edition*

Beautifully

INTERRUPTED

Beautifully

INTERRUPTED

WHEN *God* HOLDS THE PEN THAT
WRITES YOUR *story*

TERESA SWANSTROM ANDERSON

WORTHY®
PUBLISHING

Published by Worthy Books, an imprint of Worthy Publishing Group, a division of Worthy Media, Inc., One Franklin Park, 6100 Tower Circle, Suite 210, Franklin, TN 37067. WORTHY is a registered trademark of Worthy Media, Inc.

Helping people experience the heart of God

eBook available wherever digital books are sold.

Cataloging-in-Publication Data is on file with the Library of Congress.

Printed in the United States of America

18 19 20 21 22 lsc 8 7 6 5 4 3 2 1

TO MOM AND DADDY

• • • • • • • • • • • • • •

You were right, life is an adventure.
I finally get it . . . and I'm all in.

Contents

· · · · · · · · · · · · ·

Foreword

...... 🦢 ......

Have you ever given yourself just one quiet moment to step back and really take a look at your life? If you are anything like me, there are moments when the truest assessment of your circumstances can be found in one of these statements: "This is not where I thought I would be" or "How did I end up here?" I have said both of these phrases more times than I can count, but the perplexing thing is that both statements have been said in such dramatically different life experiences. Like "This is not where I thought I would be, this is such an unexpectedly awesome opportunity." Or, "This is not where I thought I would be, planning a funeral for a parent at twenty years old." How is it that we find ourselves in the middle of moments where uncertainty, doubt, goodness, and hope are intertwined with such delicacy that we can scarcely differentiate one from the other? We get beautifully interrupted by moments and what we must figure out is how to surrender to the complexities.

On a fall morning a few years ago, I was talking with a college friend who said to me, "I have a friend named Teresa Anderson that I think you should reach out to. I just know you two will hit it off." At the time I didn't think much of it but when we did connect I noticed exactly what my friend was talking about. Teresa not only is a kind soul, but she is also a gifted hostess, a mom who battles for her kids, a sharer of complex stories, and the kind of friend you can spill hot chocolate on and she will still love you (I may or may not know this from experience).

Teresa, similar to you and me, began at an early age to dream about where her life would go, who she would become, all the while making predictions about what she was convinced she would never do. While plans are useful, it's when we crumple our agenda and burn it on the altar of God's unfolding timeline, that we recognize it all turns out better than we anticipated. That is why I am thrilled you picked up this book. Teresa's story and your story will weave together with such delicacy that you will find it becomes hard to differentiate her life lessons from your own, because the stories we share bind us together in unexpected ways. So, get ready, an adventure of epic proportions awaits.

In these pages you will get to see all the expectations Teresa had for herself and experience her bumps and road blocks along the way. You will experience the struggle to maintain balance as Teresa brings inspiration and beauty to many unknowns that we all experience in life. As you wrap yourself into this book you will feel the company of many of us out there also trying to understand the hardships God lays before us and why. As you look deeper into her story you will find yourself looking at your own past road blocks and start finding the beauty in them just like Teresa does in *Beautifully Interrupted*.

This book brings to life the amazing journey of being called to serve out of your comfort zone and into God's plan for your life. It's time for you to take a journey with Teresa and go from dreaming about your life to living it. Go from planning and listening to letting go of the controller and following where God is leading you. I encourage you to pick up this book, grab a notepad and pen, curl up on a cozy couch, and open your heart to the potential of becoming deeply grateful for the ways your own life has been beautifully interrupted.

Mandy Arioto
President/CEO MOPS International
Author of *Starry Eyed*
Denver, Colorado

Introduction

I'm a little pencil in the hand of a writing God,
who is sending a love letter to the world.

MOTHER TERESA

A few years ago, God urged me to start journaling—to write out all the passions He placed within me and all the goals I wanted to accomplish, which He then expanded into something a thousand times more exciting than what I planned. I wrote down the good and the bad and the fears that I still held tightly as I slid back and forth between feelings of inadequacy and bravery. All that free writing so early in the morning before the sun said hello became the foundation for what now rests in your hands.

I learned long ago that we have an exciting God who loves to send us on adventures to fulfill our part of His high purpose—there is something specific about ourselves He wants us to understand and embrace and embody. Psalm 46:5 (NIV) says, "God is within her, she will not fall; God will help her at break of day." This doesn't mean our purpose on earth, Christ's plan for us, is always simple or easy. But it does mean He is always with us as we maneuver in and through our God-shaped adventure.

Do you trust Him enough to make the leap?

My grandparents lived in a little house built in the early 1900s that rested at the top of Queen Anne, a well-loved Seattle neighborhood with roots as deep as the hydrangeas in the front yards. In the dining room, the nearly floor-to-ceiling picture windows showcased the most gorgeous eagle's-nest view of the city below. It was the perfect perch to watch boaters parade by on Lake Washington in rain or shine (a little rain doesn't bother Seattleites) and my favorite place to watch fireworks on the Fourth of July. On the windowsill sat a small, light version of binoculars, known as a monocular, and it fit my small hands well. This one-eyed version was my favorite as a child, and my brother, Erik, and I called it a periscope, one that freed our imaginations to soar. We pretended we were pirates looking for treasure as we learned how to focus in on a boat or the opening of the Fremont Bridge below. Closing one eye and bringing the device to the other, we'd see nothing but blurry scenes. Yet with a few twists of our wrists, it all came into clear focus, so close that we'd reach out expecting to touch it.

This is how I see God's hand in the callings He's given me. At first I see nothing but blur and haze as I struggle to view what I want to see. And then His strong hand turns that little knob and everything becomes perfectly clear.

In Genesis 1:3, God said, "Let there be light," and those four words continue on today in my life and yours. Light will never be pushed away and fail to shine on the earth. The ocean will never forget how far it's allowed to come and flood the entire earth.

And God will never forget the plan He designed you for when He knit you in your mother's womb. Out of every place in this beautiful world and out of every point in our earth's history, you are here now.

For a reason.

We have this one wild and precious life—let's live it fully as God envisioned at the beginning. The Bible so aptly includes the story of Esther, a common girl who suddenly found herself queen, who was born "for such a time as this" (Esther 4:14 NIV) as she was strategically placed in the unique position to save her people. And you, too, sweet friend, were born for such a time as this.

> Out of every place in this beautiful world and out of every point in our earth's history, you are here now.

God allowed certain experiences in my life to expand my love for Him into a full-blown passion. Life changed in a way that only He could orchestrate through pouring His power into my life. God and I still chuckle together about how He is changing my fears into passions and my "I'd never" moments into "I can't get enough" experiences. If you've ever woken up one morning feeling that God may be asking more of you, then I pray He speaks to you through my story.

Allow Christ to adjust your monocular as He brings your calling and future into focus. Grab another cup of coffee and settle in as we learn together what exactly His calling means for each of us.

PART ONE

Born for Such a Time as This

CHAPTER 1

A Different Kind of God

Plastic gods are safe. Plastic gods don't mess with you.
Plastic gods don't matter much; they fit in a small crevice
of the life you want, the life you were planning to have.
And when everything in life is working . . .
plastic gods feel like enough.

JENNIE ALLEN

Somehow I had gotten comfortable with a life that was typical, ordinary, average. I was content in the simple and familiar. Without realizing it, my dreams and goals only went far enough to ensure my little boat wasn't rocked.

I was graduating from high school and felt the surge we all feel during that exciting season—that the world was my oyster. I was ready for a summer of fun before heading to college and was perfectly happy in the little bubble I lived in. My planned major made sense to me, as did the sunshiny life I was designing, the kind devoid of challenge and discomfort. The one where I married my high school boyfriend and we rode off into the sunset.

In this idealized vision, I had no desire for adventure and whispered to myself that it was not the kind of life I wanted, even though my parents always used the word *adventure* as I grew up. To me, adventure required stretching and being out of my comfort zone, like when we lived in Guatemala during my junior high years. I'd had plenty of that and I was done, thankyouverymuch.

What I didn't realize as I turned my back on adventure was that I had unwittingly turned my face toward safety and ordinary—and I was just fine living that way. So, when my parents wanted to swoop up our family and fly off on a big family trip to Europe instead of letting me go on my idea of a senior trip to Hawaii, I begged and pleaded for them to reconsider. I wanted to spend a few weeks lying on the beach, leafing through magazines and devouring novels. Despite my protests, they chose Europe.

I was so disappointed. I know, what kind of person is disappointed in an all-expenses paid trip to Europe? Looking back, I could kick my teenage self.

My dad is an academic, and to him learning is fun, so Europe was ideal. Now I would agree, but back when I was eighteen I just couldn't see learning as entertainment or enjoyment. School was hard for me, and my grades never reflected my desire to be a successful student. I envied my friends who would spend their senior trips in tropical places where the sun always shines and stress fades away with the tide. At least they were getting tan.

Instead, my family flew first into Frankfurt, Germany, where we rented the tiniest of tiny cars, and my brother, Erik, and I enjoyed days full of knees shoved up to our chins in the backseat. We drove through Germany, Austria, Switzerland, Italy, and France, and ultimately rode through the Chunnel and into England.

What happened on that trip, a trip I dug in my heels so deeply against, completely surprised me. Suddenly history came alive when we stayed in thousand-year-old castles-turned-hotels, walked over the same cobblestoned streets the Romans marched on, and searched ruins, museums, and the countryside.

I came alive.

Soaking up every morsel of history and culture I could while I munched on baguette and cheese in Italy, I walked through the narrow streets, passed over mossed canals in Venice, and fell in love. Not with a boy, but with learning and people and God. My heart awakened as it tuned in to the achingly beautiful violin music drifting through the cramped streets of this ancient, sinking land.

This dreamy *città* captivated me as deeply romantic-sounding songs drifted up to our room from the gentleman who delivered black olive scones and feta spinach tarts to our bed-and-breakfast every morning before light had peeked through our shutters. And afternoons—post-siesta, naturally—brought us the most melodious tenor from another man as he collected garbage from cans resting beneath a web of linens drying on the lines strung through the windows, high above.

I was utterly enchanted.

Love and Truth meet in the street,
Right Living and Whole Living embrace and kiss!
Truth sprouts green from the ground,
Right Living pours down from the skies!
Oh yes! GOD gives Goodness and Beauty;
our land responds with Bounty and Blessing.
Right Living strides out before him,
and clears a path for his passage.
Psalm 85:10–13 MSG

Love and Truth meet in the street.

Christ certainly allowed these two to meet me right there in the ancient streets of Europe as He showed His goodness and beauty to me in a big way. Touring small villages fenced in by nothing but countryside, our car was repeatedly delayed, surrounded by goats and sheep herded by children who had been taught by their fathers and their fathers before them.

Those children made me realize how I wanted to be taught by my Father too. I wanted Him to show me how to live a life that would yield harvest, bounty, and blessing. Though that thought frightened me because it seemed to hold adventure, it somehow made me feel safe at the same time, because I knew God would travel beside me.

As the countryside whisked by, wedged in the backseat of that tiny car, my mind wandered and dreamed. I pondered and remembered His protection and guidance in my past. He taught me as I listened.

Somehow as He met me in ancient European streets, God no longer existed as someone I loved simply because my parents taught me to. I've loved Jesus for as long as I can remember, and even as a child, my faith felt real and not simply a fairy tale my parents told at bedtime. I continue to feel fortunate and blessed that in our family, faith and relationship with Christ were like breathing; they were just part of who we were and how we lived. At the same time, though, since God had always been part of my story, it took this trip abroad to remind me what living and breathing with God by my side really meant.

Perhaps my growth had become stunted because I was jaded by years of Sunday school and youth group and I forgot the magnitude of what relationship with Him looked like in my everyday life. I lived a life where Jesus simply was but forgot that He also *is*. It was during this trip that Jesus ceased being the fair-haired, light-skinned Man-God I learned about on flannelgraphs in Sunday school.

Instead, I finally viewed Him for who He really is: a Man with dark skin and hair and grime beneath His fingernails, calloused hands from His trade as a woodworker, and blistered and weary feet from miles of dusty travels with His disciples. A Man with grit and passion and struggle. A Man with a deep love I could only attempt to fathom.

I could trust a Man-God who looked like this. He seemed legitimate. He felt solid. This was someone whose deep love was a small fleck of light that began to shine through the sliver of my heart recently pierced by His grit and passion and struggle. That tiny fracture continued breaking open as my will was tossed aside, and in its stead He began construction on a house He engineered.

My eyes poured over our dog-eared *Baedeker* travel guides, and I pleaded with my parents to pay the extra few dollars for a docent to take us through various museum tours, closed umbrella raised high above her head so we didn't lose sight of her in the dense crowds. I was as hungry for knowledge as I was for Parisian chocolate croissants—I just never had realized it. I became so enthralled while people watching in Paris that when a waiter came by for the third time to take our order, I realized I still hadn't looked at the menu. I was too absorbed in really seeing people for the first time . . . seeing their lives, their stories—both the individuals whose portraits lined the museum walls and those who occupied the café seats near our hotel.

I felt God whisper the words *bigger* and *more* into my heart, though I had no idea what they meant . . . other than the possibility that my safe little bubble might lose a bit of air.

I realized why my parents wanted to bring my brother and me here, on likely our last big family vacation before they became empty nesters. They wanted to open our eyes and hearts and minds to how vast the world is. They wanted to remind us how many exciting things there are to be a part of so we wouldn't get too comfortable, sequestering ourselves in the limited sphere of life that's so easy to get caught up in.

I still don't completely understand how my view of Christ changed so drastically on this weeks-long trip, but I think touring through new countries and cultures was the catalyst God used to get me out of my comfort zone and allow my eyes to open to His bigness—and the bigness of life itself.

My heart soared with life's possibilities and the future.

Because without realizing it, this journey across the globe opened in me something new. I saw life in a new way and viewed Christ as less of someThing and more of someOne. I hadn't read C. S. Lewis's *Mere Christianity* yet, but if I had, I know I would have highlighted this section in deep pink with arrows and exclamation points all over the margins:

Imagine yourself as a living house. God comes in to rebuild that house. At first, perhaps, you can understand what He is doing. He is getting the drains right and stopping the leaks in the roof and so on; you knew that those jobs needed doing and so you are not surprised. But presently He starts knocking the house about in a way that hurts abominably and does not seem to make any sense.

What on earth is He up to? The explanation is that He is building quite a different house from the one you thought of—throwing out a new wing here, putting on an extra floor there, running up towers, making courtyards.

You thought you were being made into a decent little cottage: but He is building a palace. He intends to come and live in it Himself.[1]

Fall quickly approached, as did the time to pack up all my belongings and move from life as a child to life as an adult. My heart pounded wildly as I remembered the past summer's travels. I never wanted it to end. I wanted to travel the world and see everything, examine every culture, and learn all I could from our world and the people in it.

The problem was, in every dream and plan, the main focus was *I* and *me*.

. . . .

CHAPTER 2

Planning God Right Out of My Plans

. . . . . . 🦢 . . . .

*Give me six hours to chop down a tree
and I will spend the first four sharpening the axe.*

ABRAHAM LINCOLN

That first semester in college, I thrived. My roommate, Lissy, was my other half, and we prided ourselves on the fact that our dorm room (complete with cream-painted cinder block walls) was decorated so beautifully, girls would swing by from other areas of campus just to check it out. It was, I believed, confirmation that I should continue forward in what I'd planned to major in for several years: interior design.

The problem was, I learned early that first semester, that though I loved creating a beautiful ambiance for myself to enjoy, I had zero passion in doing everything required to learn about it. Plus, it never occurred to me how much math was involved in creating beautiful spaces. My mind reeling over numbers was the final nail in my imaginary interior design career coffin.

Most of my friends were either pursuing fashion merchandising or elementary education. And since being around children all day, *every day*, was about the last thing in the world I ever wanted, I thought perhaps I'd take a course or two in fashion. The History of Fashion was all that was available when I went to register and I ended up loving it. We poured through time periods such as ancient Egypt and the Byzantine Empire, studying all the way to the Tudor period, the era when the Medicis seemed to rule Italy, and beyond.

I loved learning that Napoleon ordered buttons to be attached to jacket sleeves to prevent soldiers from wiping off their runny noses and dirtying up their uniform, and so became tradition. I adored knowing that my closet holds stilettos because in the early 1700s, elaborate heels decorated with miniature battle scenes were worn by King Louis XIV of France. The king decreed that these "Louis heels" could never be taller than five inches because he wanted his to stack taller than anyone else's.

I had no idea there was so much history in something as common as a shoe or buttoned jacket sleeve.

This history thing, I decided, was kind of fun.

I proudly came home during a long weekend and announced that I was on the dean's list. We all celebrated, my parents remembering well how I struggled in high school. I was ecstatic dreaming of the future, though still having no clue what my major would end up being now that I was officially *not* doing interior design.

When it came time to register for classes for the next semester, because I had an overdue library book, which I actually couldn't even find, I wasn't allowed to register. By the time I had it taken care of, every single class I had planned on taking was full.

Except art classes. Art classes were open. After rolling my eyes at the idea of paying college tuition and yet taking three art courses in one semester, I went for it.

Through those courses, God released something else in me that I didn't know was deep inside. I knew I had some sort of creativity in my blood because of my love of decorating, baking, and playing with flowers. Because of our trip to Europe and the fun I had in History of Fashion, I knew world travel and history were budding delights for me as well.

But I never knew I was artistic. Ever.

I had enjoyed art class in elementary school, sure. Who didn't love crafting buildings from stacked toothpicks and whittling stamps from potatoes? But between my Drawing Studio, Still Life Painting, and History of Art classes, I was in complete and total heaven. It's as if everything I ever thought I loved suddenly was related. It all made sense to me. And I was surprised how natural I was, paintbrush in hand.

I remember one of my professors, Michael, telling me, "Paint what you see, not what you know" like it was yesterday. In the art building, you were allowed to call your professors by their first names. We were progressive like that.

I've thought of Michael's advice hundreds of times through the years. And I don't mean only when holding a pencil or paintbrush. It whispers in my ear when I'm in a new situation or decision, when I'm traveling, or when seeing something beautiful God has created.

Paint what you see, not what you know.

What, in this moment, do you see? Forget what your brain is telling you from past experiences, hurts, failures, or weaknesses. What is Christ showing you right now? What is He impressing upon your heart? How is this situation going to be one of growth as you cultivate your relationship with Him?

Imagine this scenario and let your mind wander . . .

You're sitting in a park, cross-legged on the grass, with a large sketch pad resting in front of you, near your knees. In your hand a pencil is sharpened and ready. Glancing around, your eyes fall on a heavy-leafed tree slightly to your left. Putting the lead to the thick paper, you start drawing. With quick, sharp lines, you begin the makings of a tree and the shadow it gives on the ground below. You look up and realize your drawing looks nothing like the tree and the shadow. You didn't capture it or even the essence of it. Not because you're not artistic, but because you drew the tree and branches and leaves how your mind said they should be formed, how you wanted to see it.

Look again. Look at the colors. There's more to the tree than you initially perceived. The base of the trunk isn't simply brown as you'd first seen. The light bouncing off the grass gives small portions of it a greenish tint. And the leaves aren't just green. Depending on how the sun is hitting them, they're green with a touch of white. Or with a touch of yellow. The leaves in the shadows might have a blueish hue to them or look a flat gray.

The branches of the tree don't simply grow straight out like you had originally sketched but instead lightly curve upward . . . a few may even grow in a manner that doesn't resemble the others.

Now that you're taking the time to really look at the tree, you notice one branch twists slightly, giving the shadow a slight turn also. And the texture: it's not a smooth or flat surface. We couldn't cut out this tree using a piece of construction paper like we did when we were young and do it justice. If we tried, we would miss the real composition: the balance of delicate beauty with a rough and seemingly flawed outer covering.

Getting up and walking closer, you find there's so much more texture than you feel you're able to capture with merely pencil and paper, so many more layers and activity and seemingly imperfect or boorish qualities in its appearance. But reaching out and placing your hand upon those imperfections, you realize they show uniqueness, not ugliness. That texture shows character.

That is what it means to "paint what you see, not what you know." See the cracks and breaks. See the rings of growth. Notice the different colors and shapes, how branches intersect and offshoot. This is us, and this is how we need to view our life written by God, our Creator.

Look at your life as one of creativity and originality, acknowledging that there will be offshoots and redirections. There will be blemishes in our base that have healed over so we can continue growing. With roots growing deeper and deeper like a tree, our depth far exceeds our height and breadth.

Sometimes we are broken so we may be bound up. Realizing our scars can have more purpose than simply as reminders of past pain, our messes become our message. As I spent time praying that God would continue to give me new eyes to see Him as I pondered my future, I began seeing things come together as unrelated passions linked arm in arm, because His hand connected the dots.

Offshoots and redirections are part of my story because as He continued filling in the blanks, I realized those hard or confusing times were also what gave me strength. Everything was with purpose.

"Give in to God, come to terms with him
and everything will turn out just fine.
Let him tell you what to do;
take his words to heart.
Come back to God Almighty
and he'll rebuild your life."
Job 22:21–23 MSG

...🦢...

Viewing slides and videos of ancient reliefs, hieroglyphics, tomb paintings, and gold jewelry in my 8:00 a.m. History of Ancient Egypt class, I sat on the edge of my seat, scribbling down every detail into my ever-growing notebook. Sitting in the dimly lit room didn't put me straight to sleep like most of my classmates; instead, it invigorated me. The professors I studied under brought to life paintings, sculptures, reliefs, frescos, and so much more as they recognized symbolism and shared what was happening in culture and society at the time. Lectures, slideshows, and videos opened my eyes to topics and details I had no idea I'd find so interesting. Things like why certain sculpture or painting styles were considered brazen, how the *Salon de Paris* controlled so much of what was recognized as art, and why only particular colors of paint were allowed to be used until Monet broke all the rules and did his own thing. I looked forward to completing a thirty-page essay on a single painting or artist and fell in love with writing as the words flowed from my heart to my fingertips with relative ease. Writing about all the behind-the-scenes aspects of art energized me—I couldn't get enough.

> Realizing our scars can have more purpose than simply as reminders of past pain, our messes become our message.

I had found my "thing," I concluded! I would go on and get

my master's, then my doctorate. I would work as a curator in some magnificent museum in Europe, because Europe was where my heart resided. I would live an international life, sharing Jesus with the art world.

I had it all figured out.

But I misinterpreted the art that was my life's story. What I failed to see was that just because I had found a passion did not mean God was revealing that to me so that I would dedicate my life to art.

My budding adoration of art and writing, and love of learning about cultures and history were the avenues the Lord used to open my eyes to a larger world than what I previously saw in my modest little suburban life. He asked me to follow Him on a divergent road, for a greater purpose than I once imagined.

But hindsight is always 20/20, right?

I was so excited to be doing big things for God that I ran ahead of Him. I bolted down the road like an excited puppy, bounding in and out of bushes, distracted by anything shiny. He stood patiently waiting for me to discover that I'd left Him behind, but it took me a little while to realize I had. I was having so much fun dreaming up an amazing life *for* Him that I forgot it's only amazing if it's designed *by* Him.

Even those of us who wouldn't consider ourselves to be "planners" often fall into the trap of expectations. I'd love to know who started this movement and thought it was a good idea to have a five-year plan and a ten-year plan. Don't get me wrong, I completely understand that we have an obligation as adults to be organized, to be prepared, and to think ahead. We're to be responsible, after all . . .

But when did we get too busy planning our lives that we planned God right out of it all?

First Chronicles 22 tells the story of King David wanting to build a temple for the ark of the covenant. Looking around at his luxurious palace, it bothered him that his house was built of beautiful cedar, and yet God's house was a simple tent.

The disparity distressed him.

His plan was a noble one of designing, crafting, and building.

There was nothing wrong with David's plan. Like mine, it was a good plan. He wanted to give God a beautiful house. I wanted to reach individuals in the art world for Him.

But there was a problem with both arrangements: neither of us asked our Father what *He* wanted. What *His* thought was in the matter. Both David and I neglected to bring our excitement before Him *first*.

Our Father in heaven actually has a plan for each of us! Think on that statement for a moment. Christ placed us on this earth for a very specific purpose. Esther's uncle encouraged her in that very thing: "And who knows but that you have come to your royal position for such a time as this?" (Esther 4:14 NIV).

> But when did we get too busy planning our lives that we planned God right out of it all?

Esther, though very special, isn't completely unique. She's not the only one who was born at a precise time in history for a particular reason. You are too. And so am I. Take that concept in for a moment and sit up a little straighter after you've let it sink in. Walk a little taller. Let it put a skip into your step.

The God of the *universe* created *you* to live within this time in history because it is *now* that He has a perfect purpose for you.

I can hardly wrap my mind around that, can you?

Jeremiah 29:11 (NIV) says, "'For I know the plans I have for you,' declares the LORD, 'plans to prosper you and not to harm you, plans to give you hope and a future.'"

I'd heard that passage a million times. In high school I probably had it written in my notebook, surrounded by multicolored hearts and stars, and scribbled a bubbly lettered "Yes!" next to it in the margin of my Bible.

But just because you get something doesn't mean you really, truly *get* it.

God had some work to do until this verse actually sank in.

CHAPTER 3

An Impact That Outlives Myself

*When I stand before God at the end
of my life, I would hope that I would not have a
single bit of talent left, and could say,
"I used everything You gave me."*

ERMA BOMBECK

As college graduation grew closer and closer, I began contemplating where I wanted to continue my studies in art history, working toward my master's and eventually my doctorate. The streets of the Queen Anne neighborhood near where I lived became my place of peace and rest. I parked my car blocks away from my favorite spots to sit and read my Bible so I could wander through the beautiful old streets and enjoy God's goodness and the beauty of all He created.

I walked, prayed, dreamed, and wondered what my future would hold.

Looking back, it was such a sweet and simple time of growth. This probably sounds silly, but I'd often slide into my favorite little black dress, reminiscent of something Audrey Hepburn would wear, don my equally Audrey-esque shades, grab my Discman (please tell me you remember what that is!) with a Billie Holiday or Frank Sinatra CD inside, and be on my way.

This was how I'd spend several days a week, quietly playing my theme music because my heart was blooming and falling deeper in love with Christ, and this was my way of folding into it. This was my way of worshipping Him as I realized for the first time that worship could take many forms and needn't be boxed into simply sitting in a church pew on Sunday morning while singing hymns and choruses. This was how I embraced our time in stillness and conversation together, entwining myself in His beauty and creativity through the sights, smells, and sounds He created. Walking in the drizzling rain most days (welcome to the Northwest), coffee in hand, bag heavy with the weight of my Bible and prayer journal on my shoulder, and a light heart knowing God had big things in store for my little life.

A bench overlooking the Space Needle at Kerry Park or a cozy spot in Parsons Gardens became places I'd sit in stillness with Him. Here, God whispered to me and impressed things upon my heart. I knew I wanted a life out of the ordinary, though I was searching for what that really meant. I knew what I was passionate about and what my heart desired. But was that *truly* God's best for my life? Did I actually embrace the idea that God's plans for my life were so awe-inspiring and greater than I ever could imagine that I could *fully and honestly* give it all to Him?

Could I release my plans and let Him rewrite my story?

On sunny days when I didn't have to work, I'd often ride the ferry to my favorite little waterfront towns to grab a scoop of ice cream. Introvert that I am, I adore being by myself and in my own thoughts without distraction. I'd sit on the deck of the ferryboat, above where the cars parked, and read novels or dive into my Bible. God continued working, ever so slowly, on my heart during these times of silence and rest.

> *Now therefore, stand and see this great thing*
> *which the LORD will do before your eyes.*
> 1 Samuel 12:16 NKJV

How could I pray to make an impact on the world, yet not search for God's deepest desire for me?

Sure, I could do great things for furthering God's kingdom here on earth with the life I had planned out for myself. Mighty things. And I may have, but it wasn't about that. There was nothing wrong in what I was dreaming to do—the problem lay in the fact that I made my decision *for* Him, without it actually occurring to me to consult Him in the matter.

Many are the plans in a person's heart,
but it is the LORD's purpose that prevails.
Proverbs 19:21 NIV

Finally, one day as I sat on my favorite wooden park bench looking out over the Space Needle, the ferryboats dreamily floating from downtown Seattle to the San Juan Islands caught my eye. The dichotomy of the hustle of the city and the smooth, serene journey of the boat spoke to me. *Which life am I after?* I thought. I knew there had to be more than the hustle of life I was planning for myself.

Oh Lord, how I want to make an impact in the world for You that outlives myself, I prayed.

That day, while looking out at the sparkle of the sun upon the waves as ferryboats cut through the choppy waters, I basked in my surroundings. Listening first only to the sound of seagulls and the hubbub of a thriving city below, the words *more* and *bigger* flooded back into my mind. I heard God's still, small voice, not because He had started talking, but because I had slowed down enough to listen.

Exhaling slowly, I closed my eyes and opened my hands.

"Send me."

I whispered those words into the crisp Seattle air. To where? I had no idea. To do what? I was not yet told. But I knew it must begin with faith and trust. I liked the idea of trusting God and had placed my hope in Him since I was small, but this was different. This was intangible and big and weighty.

I didn't wake up the next morning knowing God was going to flip my life upside down in the best way possible, but little by little, Christ began shifting my priorities and allowing me to dream a little bigger. And then bigger still. Somehow, I became comfortable with being very uncomfortable. I no longer lived a life of safety, nor did I have life all figured out. In fact, as I began to embrace uncertainty and mystery and discomfort, my relationship with my heavenly Father intensified and engulfed me in an all-out fire. Lack of safety and joy somehow went hand in hand as I had begun to say yes to Him, giving God control of more than just the little things in my life.

Don't get me wrong, I was scared to death. I still am. But over and over, God has opened my eyes and heart to evidence in the Bible of other ordinary people who have also told Him, *Yes* and *Send me* to prove I'm not alone in my fear and reluctance. Even when things seem simply too big for little ol' me.

. . . 🦢 . . .

We need to find God, and he cannot be found
in noise and restlessness. God is the friend of silence.
See how nature—trees, flowers, grass—grows in silence;
see the stars, the moon and the sun, how they move in silence. . . .
We need silence to be able to touch souls.
Mother Teresa

We need to add in a time of silence and softness to balance our spirit as the noise of life consumes. Driving with the radio turned off, silencing my phone, and refraining from clicking on the television for background noise are things I do now that my life is bustling and loud. But whether your current season of life feels chaotic or simple, know it is during times of quiet that we can hear God speak.

Fight against the idea that multitasking every moment of every day is how we grow best. Admittedly, I often have Audible reading a book to me while I go about daily tasks. I feel like I'm really getting things done if I can clean the house while Priscilla Shirer reads *Fervent* to me. I love learning about things while doing the mundane tasks of life. Doing laundry while learning about the armor of God or cleaning the bathrooms while learning to pray with the power of

Christ helps keeps my mind active. It's good, yes. It's even excellent. But it shouldn't be constant.

There is so much to be learned as we remove distractions and simply spend time in solitude with Christ. We learn first what we think of ourselves, whether we're comfortable with who we are or not. Or perhaps we're reminded of the ugliness and imperfections we try to drone out with the blaring of life. It also allows Him to talk to us. To speak to our hearts. Imagine being alone with God. No distraction of radio or television. No agenda. Just being together. Does the idea of this make you anxious? Or does it appeal to you? If it makes you squirm in your seat as you wipe sweaty palms onto your jeans, pray that God would reveal to you why it makes you uncomfortable. Maybe He's trying to get your attention and wanting you to work through some things.

> *If you're lonely when you're alone, you're in bad company.*
> Jean-Paul Sartre

The Bible tells the life story of Moses, a founding father, so to say, of the lineage of Christ. Moses brought the Israelites out of Egypt, only to realize Pharaoh had changed his mind and was now chasing the former slaves and filling the horizon with Egyptian chariots and their drivers. The Hebrew people looked before them and saw nothing but a massive expanse of water in the way of their freedom. The Red Sea is far more ocean-seeming than a stream river or lake. This incredible body of water is roughly 170,000 miles long, 220 miles wide, and at its maximum depth, 7,254 feet.[2] When I grew up hearing the story of God parting the Red Sea, it never occurred to me that it is as massive as it actually was at the time Moses and the Israelites walked up to its shores.

Do you know what Moses told the Israelites when they grew angry at both God and Moses for bringing them to this place of supposed slaughter? Exodus 14:14 (NIV) says Moses reminded them, "The LORD will fight for you; you need only to be still."

The Lord will fight for you.
You need only to be still.

Today's society teaches us it's counterproductive to be still. But this verse reminds us how untrue that can be—we are not wasting time; we're being fought for. The Hebrew word for "will fight" that is used in this verse is *lacham*, which also means "to wage war, to engage in battle, to overcome, and prevail."[3] I take this to say that when we're silent and still before the Lord, Satan tries to whisper in our ear and attempts to remind us of our inadequacies, our mistakes, our failures. And if he can't get us that way, he will force our minds to swirl with all the tasks of life: to-do lists, tasks for work, things with the family, an ever-constant stream of activities we need to remember or accomplish.

That's why God *lochem* (presently fights) for us. He's fighting off and waging war against Satan's attacks on our minds because being distracted will keep us from hearing Him. But remember, *lacham* also translates to *overcome* and *prevail*. We need to continue praying in this time of silence, be consistent in our time of prayer, and wait patiently for Him to impress something onto our hearts, for Him to speak. Even when we're standing before something as daunting and frightening as the Red Sea, in a time when we feel we need to act or react, we need first to be still.

Be still before the LORD and wait patiently for him . . .
Psalm 37:7 NIV

...🦢...

When I was in middle school, my parents must have breathed a prayer to the Lord similar to the one I did decades later because suddenly our belongings were packed into storage and we found ourselves living in Guatemala.

We hadn't moved as missionaries, and though we'd first visited this beautiful country as part of a medical team, my dad wasn't a doctor. A businessman and entrepreneur, he was part owner of a company called Glasair, which manufactures small planes. The calling Christ had put upon his heart was to provide jobs for a deeply hurting economy in desperate need of growth. So, though we weren't sent by a church, this was most certainly my dad's mission field. He, too, desired for the Lord to use him for something that outlived himself.

The dreams and purpose put into the hearts of my parents would only make a small impact on the crisis of poverty and unemployment rate worldwide, sure. Did that mean they were not doing enough? No! Every single person touched by their love and care was changed as they saw Jesus in and through each of us.

We know only too well that what we are doing is nothing more than a drop in the ocean. But if the drop were not there, the ocean would be missing something.
Mother Teresa

My parents were like candles in a dark room. Their love of Christ lit the wick of every person they touched, and as new wicks ignited, they in turn brought light to those around them: friends, family, communities. Only God knows how bright and shimmering the light in that room now radiates!

"Neither do people light a lamp and put it under a bowl.
Instead they put it on its stand,
and it gives light to everyone in the house."
Matthew 5:15 NIV

We spent the first six months in a quaint little town called Antigua, which was full of cobblestoned streets and bougainvillea spiraling itself atop high white walls. Women in native dress spread out their wares to sell, and children in matching school uniforms ran around while slurping Coca-Cola through a straw, holding the sandwich bag turned soda container tight so it didn't pour out and onto the dusty ground.

Erik and I shared a room in our tiny two-bedroom cottage. His side of the wooden-walled space was full of LEGO bricks and Micro Machines; mine was plastered with posters of Candace Cameron and a baby-faced Leonardo DiCaprio from his *Growing Pains* days. Through the windows, we could practically reach out and pick fresh avocados and some sort of lemon-lime hybrid. We'd picnic in the front yard on lush green grass, frogs jumping around us.

It was an idyllic few months, yet I often felt lonely having been ripped from sixth grade halfway through the year. Apprehension of moving to a new country whose people spoke a foreign language at a time of life when I already felt awkward waned as the single mom in the cottage next to ours befriended me. Seeing a lonely girl who had yet to find friends, she taught me to paint beautiful pansies and the Guatemalan national flower, orchids, onto fabric that she sewed into tablecloths and runners. She encouraged me to keep trying when my flowers bore evidence that they were done by the hand of a child while I swooned over hers. Her English was excellent, and she'd quiz my Spanish tenses while explaining the use of different brushes and how simple flicks of the wrist turned acrylic paint into petals, stems, and leaves.

Erik and my favorite place to play was in the ruins of an old cathedral that had been destroyed in a massive earthquake in 1773. Yet through that devastation and several more that shook the country in the two hundred years that followed, our cathedral remained, and we'd happily clamber atop the crumbling portico, long since collapsed. We'd duck under the signs that said *¡Prohibido El Paso!* and pretend we didn't read enough Spanish to know what the Do Not Enter sign meant. I'm sure many a tourist caught their breath watching us jump across the apse, high above their heads. But to us, the town was our playground.

One day while a Guatemalan friend was watching us so my mom could go to the market without little ones underfoot, Erik and I played yet again at this favorite cathedral. Climbing places we shouldn't have been, as we often did, my brother jumped across a section and realized, too late, that the shrubbery he was leaping onto had grown atop itself and there was no ground beneath his feet. I caught his hand just in time, grunting and sweating as I pulled him back up, knowing the massive fall would likely break his body . . . or worse. Somehow that little scare didn't stop us from our favorite pastime as we pinkie-promised not to tell Mom and Dad and continued in our exploration, wanting nothing more than to be the adventurers we saw in our mind's eye.

Dad had his own daily adventure as he had to take the hour's drive to the capital, Guatemala City, every day to set up business. So down the mountainside he went, surrounded by the bold and colorfully painted buses loaded high with produce, goods, people, and even livestock. We always watched them go by in wonder that this was real life, that these ancient school buses turned public transportation carried so many people that they literally dangled from every side of the vehicle. And somehow they lived to ride again the next day.

With Dad in *la Ciudad* (Guatemala City) during the week, the rest of us remained in Antigua for classes. In an effort to learn Spanish quickly, my mom, Erik, and I took those same colorful buses—complete with chickens roaming the aisles and boxes roped high up top—to language school. We spent our weekdays outside in a garden on the grounds of the Lutheran Center, squeezed into small wooden desks and surrounded by the songs of tropical birds and the sight of brilliantly colored flowers that seemed to spring up overnight.

After those six months in Antigua, my dad found and remodeled the perfect space that wouldn't require any more commute. After papers were signed for a white cinder block and curved steel-roofed hangar at La Aurora International Airport, the factory had a new home . . . and so did our family. As strange as it sounds, if you ever fly into Guatemala City, you will taxi by my old home.

The windows of our second-floor bedrooms looked down to the manufacturing plant, and the smell of resin still floods my mind with long-forgotten memories. Across a small street in front of our hangar was the Guatemalan Army base, and the international runway served as our backyard.

We went to school at the Christian Academy of Guatemala (CAG), which was one of the two English-speaking schools in the city and was largely filled with missionary kids. But we also met and became friends with children whose parents worked in the embassy, and others, like us, whose parents were there for business. Since there were no school buses, several families who lived near us in Zona 13 chipped in and hired a driver, a very kind and patient man. It sounds way more glamorous than it was, and we often rode with the windows open because eight or more of us piled into the tin can of a van without air-conditioning made for lots of sweating and stinking. Suspension was another thing our van seemed to be without, and we bumpily rode over potholes and cracked pavement to and from school.

It wasn't until years later that I found out he was actually our bodyguard.

This was the mid-1990s, and it was a time of great suffering for Guatemala, economically and politically. While we lived there, two *coup d'états* occurred that violently and illegally overthrew the government. We felt personally tied to these events since the president who was ultimately overthrown had cut the ribbon at my dad's company's grand opening ceremony.

As a child, I couldn't fully understand the gravity of how we lived and what we experienced. Looking back now, I believe God shielded Erik and me from grasping the magnitude of all that we saw. And we saw truly terrible things. Guerillas were a very real threat, so machine gun–carrying guards were posted outside the entrance of our church. All of the church ushers hid firearms under their suit jackets too. Just in case.

It's hard to wrap your head around how we were able to live among all of the violence and instability. And this may sound very strange if you've never lived in such an environment, but it wasn't that big of a deal. Or rather, it was a *huge* deal, but it was something you just learned to live with. You were careful, took precautions, and completely trusted in God to keep your family safe, praying for Him to tell you when enough was enough and it was time to leave.

When we did leave, we left quickly, leaving behind most of our possessions. I'm not even sure what happened to our cats or that massive blue-painted hand-carved table in our kitchen. We carried just a suitcase full of clothes and a handful of precious items. We said only a few good-byes.

I thought we had fled the country because of devastation guerillas wreaked in our little community. But years later, my parents told us that, in fact, we left because there was a hit out on my dad.

Even before living in Central America, my parents began infusing a love of our world into Erik and my lives. We would eat at restaurants that served Thai, Indian, or Scandinavian cuisine. They brought friends into our lives who were from all over the world. And though we weren't able to trot across the globe physically, we often had tickets for an event at the Seattle Opera house called World Cavalcade.

I loved these special evenings at World Cavalcade because not only did I get to dress up and stay out late, but a screen was put in place in the middle of the elegant and gilded stage that usually housed ballets and operas. These narrated travel films from around the world presented me with life and cultures I fell in love with. Sitting in the velvet seats of the opera house, we would travel across the world to India, Egypt, Brazil, and Italy. We'd view life in England or cities throughout the Holy Land. During intermission as we sipped sparkling cider and hot chocolate, Erik and I would try out these new languages that felt funny on our tongues, exploding in laughter at the annoyed glances we'd receive from older, regal-looking men and women in their furs and suits.

I wouldn't recognize until years later that these experiences as a child helped prepare me for the day I released my plans back to God while sitting on that wooden park bench. The international life I planned for myself would be repurposed into a life that would reach much further, have a greater impact, and become much more beneficial because He was in control rather than me.

I used to think I had to act a certain way to follow God,
but now I know God doesn't want us to be typical.
Bob Goff[4]

PART TWO

A Heart Under Construction

CHAPTER 4

Character to Match the Assignment

*People do not seem to realize that their opinion
of the world is also a confession of character.*

RALPH WALDO EMERSON

When we left Guatemala and rejoined life in the States, we moved into my grandparents' house in Seattle's Queen Anne neighborhood, minutes from that green wooden park bench I would sit on and pray a decade later. My grandfather's health was failing, and we wanted to be close to him and also be there for my grandmother.

But I immediately began to struggle. Nothing made sense anymore.

Though Erik and I rejoined the life we had left years before, going to the same school we had previously attended, we wrongfully assumed friendships would pick up where they had left off.

Since this was pre-Internet, I asked my best friend one day what she thought about the letters I had sent her, if she had gotten them, because in my nearly three years away, I never received any from her.

She shrugged as her locker slammed closed and said, "Yeah, I got them. I read a little bit. But your letters are really long, ya know?"

I stared at her with a feeling of rejection I couldn't comprehend. This girl, who was supposed to care about me, couldn't even get through a few pages of what was going on in my world . . . a world away.

I then realized it wasn't that everything was different. It was that *I* was different.

I no longer fit in, if I ever did.

> *Some people think luxury is the opposite of poverty.*
> *It is not. It is the opposite of vulgarity.*
> Coco Chanel[5]

School became a struggle. Listening to shockingly crass and foul conversations from my fellow classmates and wading through surface-level friendships exhausted me. I finally found some girls who were authentic and wanted to make a difference in this world and who loved Jesus deeply. I cherished them, but I could feel myself still having to remove a part of who I had become: the girl who had grown up quickly by experiencing how much of the world lives.

This American life, I realized, is simply not real life.

But over time I allowed myself to morph back into the girl who thought mostly of friends, clothes, and boys. One who was no longer shocked by superficial conversation, waste, and excess. Deep down, I knew God had something bigger planned for me, but I pushed the bigness out of my mind. I was always in student leadership and wanted to do what I could to "change the world," but even that evolved into mostly liking the *idea* of change. I didn't actually want to get my hands dirty.

Mere weeks before summer ended and my junior year of high school began, my parents decided it would be healthy for Erik and me to switch to public school. *Changing schools again?* I thought. *No. Not happening. No more new. I'm done. I just want to settle in. I want to be comfortable. I'm sick of new and tired of feeling stretched all the time.*

This would be my fourth school in my middle and high school years. Well, five if you counted the brief attempt at homeschooling when we initially moved to Guatemala. I fought and cried and screamed. But Mom and Dad held firm, knowing the importance of what the Lord had impressed upon their hearts.

Many things about our Christian school were difficult for me and sort of a by-product of being at a private school. But the Bible knowledge and the strong foundation of Christ's love I learned within those walls undeniably prepared me for living out my faith once I stepped foot in public school. Public school grounded me—and I loved it. Time and time again I was faced with decisions that clarified for me whether I truly believed my faith to be truth or not. I was made fun of, challenged, and debated with. It was as if new friends watched to see if I'd slip up . . . if I truly believed what I claimed. As my last two years of high school sped by, these friends realized my words and my actions seemed to line up—not that I was perfect all the time, I was far from that—but they saw enough consistency that their trust in me emboldened the trust and confidence I had in God.

God was still shaping me and adjusting my worldview during this time. Though I had grown a lot from my experiences, I was still scared of the big world and wasn't sure of my place in it. I prayed against being used somewhere like Africa whenever we raised money for missionaries or heard someone speak about the work they did there. When did I stop being this girl who embraced adventure and thrill, seeing it as an opportunity to live freely and instead viewed it as too risky?

I think God just chuckled to Himself.

Years passed and I grew from a girl with big dreams for herself into a young woman who desired God's big dreams instead. Seasons came and went following the day I sat on that park bench and handed God back the pen that would write my life's story. I'd held back from continuing my higher degrees in art history because I'd felt a weighty *no* from Him. Not knowing what was next, I tried my best to be patient while waiting for God to reveal more of His plan to me, but I struggled in the wait.

Working in two sister restaurants on Seattle's waterfront all through college earned me the title of comanager of one of the restaurants a year after graduation. I loved that my restaurant was full of friends new and old that I'd helped hire, train, and encourage. This place was a launching pad for young dreamers who had big aspirations in graphic design, film, and the medical field. Feeling a bit stuck in the interim, I knew God would use this place as a launching pad for me too. I tried my best to swallow down my own disappointment and keep a genuine smile on my face as coworkers handed me their notice before heading to grad school, flying to New York for internships, and spending a summer with the Peace Corps. Feeling doomed to live a small life, I fumbled with the sting of defeat as I recalled the international life I had lived as a child and the one in the art world I had previously planned.

Growing up in Seattle meant I had a deep affection for the sea and being near it filled me with hope. My throat would tighten from holding back tears every time I walked onto the patio of the restaurant, praying Christ would sweep a thick salt-watery breeze over me and rustle my hair. I loved thinking of Him in the water and in the wind. I loved spending my days so close to docked sailboats in the harbor that I could hear their ropes creaking as the tide tried to take them back out. Sometimes I felt like I was one of those glossy white vessels, tied up and unable to get far. Wanting God to use me for what I was created for, my heart ached to get out of the safe life I lived. It didn't even occur to me that I used to *want* a safe, smallish life. By giving me what I once wanted, God was helping me realize I was made for more.

I never tired of walking upstairs and into the dining room of the fancier of the two restaurants and seeing the sweeping panorama of the Elliott Bay. The view never ceased to take my breath away. God always breathed new life into my soul as I stood before those windows that boasted a grand stretch of boat, sea, and sky. He was with me in my wait. Even when the wait went longer than I wanted it to.

With a sore and melancholy spirit, I watched the web of masts bobbing to and fro with the rippling of the waves and realized this quote by J. A. Shedd was true: "A ship in harbor is safe, but that's not what ships are built for."

I knew security and control were what I ultimately craved. I had no idea what leaving my safe harbor would mean; the idea of living outside my comfort zone sent shivers down my spine. God continued to whisper the word *more* into my very core. My heart began to race as I thought back to the day I'd opened my hands to Him and asked Him to direct my path with the words *Yes* and *Send me* playing upon my lips. He hadn't forgotten about me. Somehow there was something to be learned in this time of anticipation.

As my mind recalled the day on the bench that overlooked the Space Needle, it became abundantly clear that there wasn't much choice. Either I was going to trust Him enough to go with Him, or I wasn't. I needed to quit telling God to hurry up and not only angle myself toward Him with the idea that He actually had His own story for me, but realize that He'd already started penning it down.

Looking through an old journal from during this time of wait, I found this:

How long was it from the time that God first spoke to Abram (Abraham) that Isaac, the child of promise, was born? Twenty-five years! (see Genesis 12:4 & 21:5)

Why did God wait twenty-five years? Because it took God twenty-five years to make a father suitable for Isaac. God was not concerned so much about Abram, but about a nation.

The quality of the father will affect the quality of all the generations that follow. God took time to build Abram into the man of character he needed to be.

Abram had to begin to adjust his life to God's ways immediately after the promise had been given. He could not wait until Isaac was born and then try to become the father God wanted him to be.

I'm reminded of the two times I tried learning the piano. The first occasion I was in elementary school, and taking lessons on campus meant once a week I had to spend recess in a tiny, musty-smelling piano room that felt no larger than a closet. In fact, I think it previously was a closet.

I wanted to learn to play the beautiful hymns and arias that my mother made look so easy as her fingers moved quickly over the keys. But it was hard! You had to actually practice (a lot!) to play that effortlessly well. So, when I broke my arm a few months into the school year, I was secretly glad and didn't try again for almost fifteen years.

Then, my junior year in college, when I needed a few electives and I saw that Piano 101 was an option, I jumped at it. I thought enough years had passed that I'd be willing to take the time for the basics and it'd be easier in general.

Nope.

I hated it. I had to relearn where middle C was and how to place my fingers. I was required to practice all the silly little songs I had learned as a child (and hated even then). I didn't want to take the time to learn what was needed in building my foundation.

Give me something that required both hands moving all over the keyboard! I'd close my eyes and imagine myself swaying back and forth to reach the farthest keys, the beautiful melodies drifting from the white baby grand that I pictured buying one day. I couldn't wait to fill the whole house with soul-stirring notes, just like my mom used to do years earlier while playing the hand-me-down upright piano in our living room.

Ultimately, I dropped the class on the last possible day to do so, knowing I simply wasn't willing to take the time to grow. I refused to learn the basics, the foundational aspects. I wanted to be Mozart from the first day I walked into class. God taught me a lesson: If I see small things as insignificant, with what heart could I take on things of greater substance and honor?

God certainly wasn't saying to me like the master said to his servants in Matthew 25:21 (ESV), "Well done, good and faithful servant. You have been faithful over a little; I will set you over much. Enter into the joy of your master."

There are so many times in life when I've decided I was ready for something and wanted to jump right in, realizing too late that I wasn't. One of my most embarrassing moments ever was auditioning for the spring musical in my senior year of high school. I'd chosen the song and monologue, practicing each a handful of times. I had romanticized it all so fully that there was no doubt in my mind I'd not only get a part but gain the lead. The day of tryouts, I froze. Never having practiced in front of anyone, standing alone on stage absolutely and totally terrified me. As all eyes were on me, the truth of my preparation (or lack thereof) showed brightly. I forgot every word of the monologue and stammered and trembled my way through the song. I didn't have a firm foundation or the needed preparation. And I crumbled in front of a hundred peers.

No matter how exciting plunging off a cliff and into a pool below seems, if we jump before learning to swim, we'll drown. We know this—it's obvious, right? So why do we forget that same concept as we jump into new experiences?

Another entry from that tattered journal from years ago reminds me that there is great purpose in waiting. I don't know where I found this piece of wisdom I recorded here. It surely wasn't my own. I wish I was that wise.

"When God called Abram, he said, 'I will make your name great.'" (Genesis 12:2 NIV)

That means: I will develop your character to match the assignment I'm giving you.

Nothing is more pathetic than having a small character in a big assignment. Many of us don't want to give attention to our character; we just want the big assignment from God.

If you can't be faithful in a little, God will not give you the larger assignment. He may want to adjust your life and character in smaller assignments in order to prepare you for the larger ones.

God finally made it abundantly clear that I needed to leave that little restaurant on the bay. I began to interview for positions at nonprofit after nonprofit, but each time it came down to myself and one other person. And every time I was the one left wanting. As the shame of inadequacy began to sneak in, I felt like God was whispering that it was not that I wasn't good enough, it was that these places were simply not where He wanted me. I couldn't ask the Lord to open doors without welcoming those that were closed, because each one I found shut tight guided me closer to the one I'd find unlocked.

Feeling renewed expectation that He really was leading the way, I continued praying as I circled ads in the classifieds and searched websites and bulletin boards. Finally, one day a friend mentioned her boyfriend's company was hiring and suggested I apply.

Knowing I needed some sort of income because bills were piling up, I interviewed while continuing to pray that God would direct my path and make His plan obvious. Surprised when I got the job, I secretly wondered how working in a cubicle could possibly be a chapter in God's story for me.

And then I met Ben.

In the couple years we worked together, we set each other up on dates with friends and roommates. I lent him my patio table and chairs when his house was being renovated and he wanted to make dinner for his then-girlfriend. He drove me to work so I didn't have to take the bus downtown, and we attended the same church, and even the same Bible study. The eight-year age difference shielded our eyes and hearts from there ever being more than friendship between us. And then all at once, without anticipating its arrival . . . a deep love for one another snuck up and crashed over us like a tidal wave.

Becoming bolder in my faith as my relationship with God grew, I felt deeply that the Lord had something unexpected for me. My ordinary, common life would be flipped around as a testimony that He can use anyone who desires to be used. Still unaware what my purpose or assignment from God was, I knew what it *wasn't*. Holding on to that, I continued forward as I worked on becoming a woman of substance. I made mistakes and frequently got in my own way, but as time continued, I realized more and more how God could use broken people and that I didn't have to be perfect to be used in His perfect plan.

> *Now when they saw the boldness of Peter and John,*
> *and perceived that they were uneducated, common men, they were*
> *astonished. And they recognized that they had been with Jesus.*
> Acts 4:13 ESV

Our heavenly Father uses ordinary men and women who love Him. He uses regular people like you and me, regardless of our feelings of inadequacy and incapability. In fact, He uses us as a *result* of them. Because along with those feelings of inadequacy is a dependence on the Lord, knowing it is not in our own strength that we do things but in *His* strength. My old plan in the art world was one I was planning to succeed in because I felt I could do it, not because I'd asked Him to work through me. My time of wait taught me to stop trying to do things in my own excellence and strive instead to do things in His.

In the Bible, young David was anointed with oil over a decade before becoming king of Israel. He, too, didn't know what he was anointed for and lived in expectation of God's plan for his life. After David killed a giant named Goliath, King Saul invited David to serve him personally, playing the harp on troubling days as well as becoming his armor bearer. What David didn't realize during that time of service to the king was that God was preparing him in ways he couldn't have orchestrated himself. What better way to learn how to be king than as a constant figure in Saul's day-to-day life? As harpist, David entered into Saul's home and gained relationships with the king's family. As armor bearer, David was required to stand by Saul's side as he spoke strategy with his generals. David saw how the king responded under stress in war, what he did when battle was successful, and how he led his people through defeat.

After being promoted to a high-ranking official in Saul's army and seeing huge success, David spent years fleeing from the jealous hand of Saul. Though David was confused and discouraged, God used this time as well. As a warrior who initially hid and tried to do things on his own merit, David transformed into someone who sought God's direction first, becoming an upright man of deep integrity whom God Himself called "a man after my own heart" (Acts 13:22 NIV). Like us, David was far from perfect. But because of his struggles and years when life seemed to be on hold, he became a man who trusted God fully. David's faith-filled mentality turned him into an incredible king with a legendary story.

> By acknowledging that there is nothing outside of His timing, we can push frustration aside through seasons of seeming pause, knowing that there is teaching within them.

David saw Saul in personal situations and how he dealt with responsibilities in work. My time in that little cubicle helped me see Ben through all sorts of seasons as well. I witnessed his humility when work went well and his character through disappointment in deals gone south. I saw him read his Bible through the little window by the door of his office as I walked down the hall, and I observed his integrity through relationships, both healthy and lousy. I saw adventure in him when he'd fly across the country to learn how to ride bulls in Kansas and barefoot water ski in Alaska.

I would have observed some of these things had we been simply friends, but not as fully as seeing him at work day in and day out. God used that little cubicle and my season of wait to grow my character and build the foundation needed before I was ready for the next open door. And He used that time to allow me to watch the same things occur in Ben.

God's top desire is for us to love Him as we live an openhanded life, seeking to join Him in what He's doing. By acknowledging that there is nothing outside of His timing, we can push frustration aside through seasons of seeming pause, knowing that there is teaching within them. Walking closely by God's side, He taught me what needed to be adjusted and strengthened me so I could continue onto the next chapter in the story He was writing. And He was doing the same with Ben.

... 🦢 ...

Our pastor, Nirup Alphonse, was recently out one Sunday and my dear friend Crystal Woodman Miller preached in his place while he healed. I promised Crystal I'd sit in the front row and both pray for her and cheer her on. Instead, it felt as if I needed to sit in that front row because it was vital I had zero distraction while the Lord used her to remind me what He was already prompting. What she said lined up so well with what I had already typed within the pages of this chapter that I dashed home and hopped on my computer to keep writing as thoughts spilled out.

> *If you are breathing, it is not without reason and possibility*
> *that Jesus can choose you and change you.*
> Crystal Woodman Miller[6]

As we strive to see honor in small assignments, I think we often assume it's only the smallish assignments we'll ever be commissioned to do. As if we are too average to be used and therefore He will pick someone better, someone more qualified for the bigger purpose or callings. I'm betting each of us can think of a dozen people with more background, experience, and aptitude for anything the Lord could possibly ask and require. Whatever it is, we think there is someone who could do it better.

But listen up, because this is important: if you're living life with a "Put me in, Coach!" mentality, He will absolutely put you in. Not because you know every play and are so amazing He'd be dumb not to . . . but because you know you don't, yet you're willing to go in anyway. The fact that I'm using even a rudimentary sports analogy is hilarious because I'm just not a sports girl. In fact, I'm the type who only loves football season because it's a chance to cuddle up to my husband on the couch and read while he watches. But you get what I'm saying, right?

It's how our hearts are positioned that matters more than the experience on our résumé. God uses the ordinary person, the average Joe and Jane. He will use us not because we have the ability, but He will give us the ability because He wants to use us.

> He will use us not because we have the ability, but He will give us the ability because He wants to use us.

As plain ol' us yields to His divine plan, His glory and power are displayed. Thing is, just because our hand is raised and we bounce in our seats with an impatient and high-strung, "Ooh ooh ooh! Choose me! Choose ME!" disposition, it doesn't mean He will deem us prepared. It's a dichotomy, isn't it? The validity and certainty of "the same God who chooses us is the same God who equips us," as Crystal reminded me that morning. But what we need to remember is the equipping is sometimes a longer process than we want or think it should be. The moment the assignment or calling is given isn't typically the same moment we step into it.

CHAPTER 5

Removing the Blinders

*I have learned that faith means trusting in advance
what will only make sense in reverse.*

PHILIP YANCEY

After finally admitting to the idea that our friendship had turned into something deeper, Ben and I found ourselves on a real date. This evening together wasn't our normal three-mile run around Green Lake followed by a scoop of ice cream or emptying pockets of quarters while playing rounds of Big Buck Hunter in the arcade attached to our favorite Thai restaurant. The night felt grown-up and important. Attending a black-tie auction in support of a dear friend's nonprofit that provides hope after domestic violence, we were swept up like Cinderella at the ball.

It was a magical kind of night where we felt God was doing big things, and without whispering it aloud, I went with expectation for Him to move. Initially brushing it off with the idea that we were joining hands with a worthy ministry or that I was simply starry-eyed and in love, my heart told me that there was something wider, that my borders were about to reach further.

I certainly didn't know what that would mean and didn't pretend to know how He'd do it, but I perceived *somehow* this season of wintery wait where my roots grew deep would soon erupt into spring. Those weeks prior to the auction, I felt on the verge of turning a corner, coming face-to-face with something Great with a capital *G*, because I knew it would be given by God Himself.

Strolling through tables filled with silent auction items we could mostly only pretend to afford, Ben and I stood before a black-and-white photograph of a little boy in Malawi, praying. With eyes closed, a sweeping of thick lashes catching the light, this sweet little boy serenely held his face to the heavens in conversation with his Creator. So taken by the photograph, we focused first on the beauty of the little boy, and then noticed all the other little faces in the background, also praying. We stood there unable to break away from the image, our feet so firmly planted that our fancy shoes seemed to have been cemented into the floor. It was like scales fell from my eyes or blinders sprang away from my face in realization of what my future would be. Ben and I had known each other for years at this point, slowly, but steadily falling in love with one another. We'd gone on unofficial "dates" and been each other's confidants for a long time, and we'd even talked about marriage before that night, mainly in passing while on one of our "hangouts" we wouldn't acknowledge as official dates. Suddenly, though, this special night felt different and through this photo, I discerned an impenetrable force urging *us* toward the idea of adoption, specifically from Africa. Not just me. But us—Ben and me, together, pursuing adoption.

With the framed portrait resting upon my lap as I sat in the passenger seat on our way home, Ben and I smiled like children whose father had given them a gift. Laughing at the idea of once never wanting children, I felt God's amusement in allowing me to see that I would still live an international life. It would just be in a different way than I had originally thought.

That night God shared part of His future story for me and I jumped into His arms knowing He was inviting me into its unfolding. By giving me an invitation to enter into His plans, I was also being invited into the chrysalis of His timing. I knew He would bring it to completion. The only question was when. Leaving one waiting period, I entered into another.

As often as I'd push away frustrated thoughts in various periods of wait, I often correlated this unwanted season with the feelings of winter: cold, barren, lifeless, and gray. What I neglected to tie together, however, was how I lived during not the theoretical winter months but the real-life ones. I don't know if it's my Scandinavian heritage or if it's just how I'm built, but for me, the chilly days when the sun sets earlier and rises again later have become a sweet time of reconnection. It's not until recently that I even knew this was a concept or that it had a name: the Danish word *hygge* (hue-guh).[7]

This concept is essentially the art of creating intimacy and building sanctuary. It's inviting a feeling of closeness while paying attention to what makes us feel openhearted and alive. Although I envision cozying up with a thick, soft blanket, reading a book next to the roaring fire or chopping vegetables and tossing ingredients into a simmering pot for a thick stew or soup, this doesn't have anything to do with what is tangible. It's nothing you can buy or an activity to do; it's purely a feeling. By living *hygge*, we slow down and create kinship while celebrating the little things in our every day. It's the ability to not simply *be* present, but to recognize and *enjoy* the present.

Can we learn to enjoy our wait?

Can we discover how to take pleasure in this pause of preparation?

If I think of *hygge* in connection to our wait, it seems to me that it's during winter, during an actual appreciation of it, that our bond with Christ grows in a way we may not have the opportunity for during other seasons. As we slow down enough to concentrate on becoming rooted in Him, we look past the lack of foliage and apparent fruit and understand the importance of this season. Without this time when we learn to abide in Him while our roots dig in deeply, the moment a storm rises up, blowing and bending us to and fro, we'll be ripped up and tossed into the rubble. Spring doesn't forget to come. It never ceases to show up, yet neither does it come before it's supposed to. Budding growth from spring's warmth will arrive when the Lord ordains it to. In this same way, our wintery wait will ultimately turn to spring's fruition in God's perfect timing.

We cannot hurry seasons along. There is no magical phrase to encourage a season's early sprouting or cause it to end prematurely. During this time of necessary wait, we need to reconsider how we position ourselves. Turning away from words like *gloomy*, *dreary*, and *somber*, let's instead appreciate it as a time of anticipation while we sit and abide in relationship with the One who knows more about perfect timing than we ever will.

Even when one wait ends, another will inevitably begin. Seasons never end, nor does the timing of His purposes. Christ removed the blinders from my eyes with the knowledge that we'd one day adopt, but He didn't give more directive or information. I've learned we're usually only given step-by-step clarity, and this revelation was all Ben and I needed to start praying differently as the next few years were spent wrapping our minds around the bigness of our epiphany.

> *For everything that happens in life—there is a season,*
> *a right time for everything under heaven.*
> Ecclesiastes 3:1 VOICE

After formally dating four months before becoming engaged, Ben and I spent another four months planning the day we'd become man and wife. To those who didn't know us well it seemed fast, but most friends just chuckled that "it was about time." Ben and I bought our first little house together, and my best friend, Kiesha, and I lived in it before our wedding day, though Ben and I spent evenings painting and scouring Craigslist for the perfect items to make it feel like a home we'd both love.

We'd found the seemingly perfect house right on Green Lake, the place where we spent our weekends eating at chic bistros, sipping coffee, and going on runs. It was the type of place where you didn't need your car because everything was in walking distance and your neighbors were all fun, young, and urban. We loved being active and outside, and after realizing this house met all our criteria, we were enchanted. In fact, I think I stopped breathing for a moment upon learning that though the home was built in 1912, it was exquisitely restored back to its original era by the previous owner—a man who worked in the restoration department at the Seattle Art Museum. It was charming and we fell in love with it, excited to spend our early years of marriage making memories within its walls.

On our honeymoon, however, God threw us a curveball. While sinking our toes into the warm Hawaiian sand, Ben answered a call saying he had received a promotion and was being transferred across the country to Texas. We were so excited that we got to go on this adventure together shortly after returning home that we packed boxes without much thought of the bigness of our move. We owned that darling bungalow a total of four months.

This cross-country move was the inauguration of the waves that were beginning to rock us out of what was comfortable. God began teaching us that though winds and storms would weather us and try to throw us off course, we had Him. We rested in the promise that God would hold us securely and that a cord built of the three of us would bind us tightly to Him, the Anchor.

As we transported our lives from Seattle to San Antonio, Texas, we moved into the home of Ben's best friend . . . along with his roommate. Leaving all our belongings in storage, including our new china and the crystal Kate Spade vase I was so excited to register for, I rid myself of all expectations of what young married life looked like. Living several months as a bright-eyed newlywed in a home with three guys and none of my own belongings taught me many things. Though I'd not have chosen this avenue for our first few months of marriage, we had fun, laughed a ton, and learned how to make Texas BBQ and the secret to great guacamole. Moreover, I learned once again that I needed to release my so-called perfect plans. My mom always says, "Blessed are the flexible, for they shall not be bent out of shape," and I learned the meaning of these words in a profound way as I spent my days in a home that wasn't my own.

When I wasn't hanging around the "bachelor pad" with my husband and new "brothers," I counseled women at a crisis pregnancy center in an area of town I normally wouldn't have felt comfortable going. Our office was in a sketchy building where cars were often broken into and vandalized. I prayed for my own safety while riding the creaky elevator and walking through the dimly lit hallway, wondering how many months it would take for someone to replace the broken bulbs. There were only a handful of ladies who volunteered there—we often ran the office alone, serving as receptionist, counselor, and pregnancy test taker all at the same time.

I had never been part of something that weighed so deeply on my heart. I remember one dark-haired thirty-something who was thin as a rail, with deep, dark circles under her eyes and wrinkles on her skin bearing evidence that she'd lived more life than her years should have told. Her children were all taken away because she struggled with addiction and found herself (and her children) on the streets to sleep. A man had given her shelter—with the payment of, well, her company. I fumbled with her pregnancy test, praying hard that the little lines didn't register on the panel. But they did, and quite quickly. As I held her hands, she sobbed. And I sobbed with her.

Saddened that these women felt so lost and angry that their situation left them feeling small and in a stalemate, I always left emotionally drained. With the knowledge that God had a plan for these women just as much as He had for me, I began praying over them by name when I was at home, as I sat in my empty office when they missed appointments, or when they went somewhere to end a pregnancy. I hated the pain in their eyes and the grief in their hearts.

Sometimes I felt them look at me as naïve and sheltered, not having experienced pain like they had. Knowing my mistakes may be different, I knew God could turn even the darkest situation around and use our bad choices for His glory. Messes could become His message, and I earnestly thanked God for allowing me to be part of each of these women's stories.

Every morning I unlocked the door, turned on the lights, and flipped the Closed sign in the window around to Open was another day He continued to work on my heart and change how I viewed children. After our experience at the auction and feeling God's urging that Ben and I would adopt, my desire to have a child or two had grown, but here, seeing the pain of the mother that was not the fault of the child, I no longer saw them as a scary, messy, loud burden, but instead saw them as a deep blessing. As I positioned myself as an advocate for these heavy-laden women, they shed scared and brave tears while sharing with me in such a vulnerable way. And with each tear, God continued breaking me and binding my love for each woman and their children in a deeper way than I could have fathomed. I prayed for adoption over women who didn't want to be mothers, or simply couldn't be in that season, and I was desperate for them to choose against ending their pregnancies. With each prayer, the notion of bringing another woman's child in as my own grew heavier inside the nooks and crannies of my soul.

> Often we believe *in* Him, but what others speak about us is sometimes louder and stronger than our trust that He can use us.

Satan's goal is for us to believe our mistakes are who we are, but they are not what define us. He shrinks our story, causing us to believe we're doomed to live a life of regret and unfulfilled dreams. Time and time again, a lonely hollowness flashed in the eyes of the women I'd sit with on the old couch in my office. Often we believe *in* Him, but what others speak about us is sometimes louder and stronger than our trust that He can use us. We forget our identity is in Christ, not in our past. The world was brought into life with God's voice, and I prayed like crazy that He'd breathe life into these women too.

Claiming the story God was writing, not simply the one I

thought I wanted, I realized growth and comfort do not comingle. Easy can't be my standard, for Jesus never asked us to live an easy life. But He has asked us to live with faithfulness and bravery. Ben and I didn't want to be people who talked about God, but rather people who lived Him. His plan and timing made no sense to us, and yet as we waited those years for Him to reveal the *when* portion of His plan, we knew we needed to enter into what He was asking. For now, the only thing we needed to do was say yes. We couldn't pray God would interrupt us, only to revoke it later because it didn't suit our agenda and timeline. We had to be willing to act, whenever the call came.

As our boat sailed even further from the safety of the harbor, we hung on tightly, reminding ourselves once again that He was indeed the Anchor that would keep us from veering off course.

I've come to realize God rarely gives us all the information and details of what He's doing, yet I long to live a life without blinders. Like top secret assignments, sometimes things are shared on a "need-to-know basis." When God opens our eyes to an assignment, it's because He's inviting us to take part in it and change the way we're living our lives so we may walk in alignment with the responsibility He's presenting.

Callings and assignments from our heavenly Father will demonstrate His nature, His provision, His strength, and His love to a watching world. My prayer is that He uses me somewhere within the pages of the story He's writing for the world.

CHAPTER 6

Releasing Expectations

*To my young friends out there: Life can be great,
but not when you can't see it. So, open your eyes to life:
to see it in the vivid colors that God gave us
as a precious gift to His children, to enjoy life to the fullest,
and to make it count. Say yes to your life.*

NANCY REAGAN

"No."

"No no no no no no!"

I watched wide-eyed from the doorway as she spilled a just-poured glass of grape juice. The glass tumbled almost in slow motion from her chubby fingers as the juice covered the family's heirloom handmade lace tablecloth, which had draped the table in brilliant white just moments before.

I spent most of the afternoon trying to keep the girls from that room for this exact reason: it was full of antiques, heirlooms, and pretty, fragile things I imagined being used as playthings and therefore broken things. But as I was trying to calm the tears of her sister, this one escaped my eye for a moment too long.

I quickly swooped in, praying I could somehow get the stain out before their parents returned home. I knew I had to tell the truth, but everything inside me screamed, *Fix it!* or I'd never babysit for them again.

But do you really want to? my mind whispered to me.

As I mopped up the deep purple dripping from every notch, crevice, and beautiful ornamental design crafted into that old table, I decided we needed to get out and go for a walk. A walk would be so much easier than telling these children not to touch so many things in their very own home. *Can you no longer have pretty things once kids enter into your family?* I wondered. *Probably not.* I shrugged. Knowing the future, God probably laughed and elbowed Jesus, both shaking their heads at me in recognition of my age, only a handful of years more than these girls in my charge for the day.

Our walk down the Queen Anne streets was beautiful as always. Hundred-year-old bungalows stretched out across each street, the green manicured lawns and gardens proudly displaying decades' worth of tender loving care, boasting yards full of hydrangeas and lilacs. Pink-hued roses dreamily winded their way through arches and trellises.

The girls began complaining of being cold in the afternoon's misty gray drizzle, so when they tugged at my shirt and my patience, we spun on our heels and headed back to their home. Reaching the front steps of the house, I put my hand into my pocket. No key.

No! I thought as my heart caught in my throat.

I fumbled in disbelief through all the pockets in my jeans and in my jacket. Nothing.

I tried the doorknob, praying it somehow turned. Nope.

We bolted around to the back and tried the door from the backyard into the kitchen.

Please, Jesus, please. Pu-leeeeeze let it open.

Locked.

I'll be honest, I thought about lifting one of these young children up through the second-story window I noticed was half-open because I didn't want to have to explain both this and the grape juice incident. I'm a firstborn! I'm responsible and capable! After looking up at the window for a moment, though, I figured even if they didn't fall to their death, they'd probably just let themselves in and ransack the place, never actually unlocking the door and letting me in. How would I explain that one?

I never babysat again . . . not that they asked me to.

Whenever I was around children, I pictured every Disney "After-school Special" and every family movie I'd ever seen where children ran wild and swung from the chandelier. I imagined boys with grubby hands, stuffing frogs and dirt pies into their pants pockets, and girls overflowing the bathtub in an effort to beautify the wild raccoon they'd found in the backyard.

I thought if I turned my back for a moment, or perhaps if I even blinked, pigtails would be chopped off in the name of beauty, fingernail polish would coat the dog's nails, and children's heads would be stuck between the rails in stair banisters.

Children scared me.

Really, really scared me.

Maybe children are like dogs or bears and can smell fear. Or perhaps they can smell great dislike. Because they didn't seem to care for me, just as I didn't care for them.

Again, I think God just shook His head and chuckled.

Instead of babysitting, I decided pet-sitting and house-sitting were more my speed. I loved taking dogs out on walks and making sure cat bowls were filled. I'd snuggle with these sweet creatures, breathing a deep sigh of relief they didn't have opposable thumbs and therefore could not work scissors or open bottles of bright-red nail polish.

When house-sitting, I'd do more than simply collect the mail. *These people with such messy children need my help,* I thought to myself. I took it upon myself not only to water their plants and feed their pets but to act as housekeeper too. They would leave on vacation with milk splattered all over the tabletop and crumbs cluttering kitchen counters. Their kids' artwork was plastered all over the refrigerator, so I was careful not to crunch it when I closed the doors. Shoes and mismatched socks cluttered the sticky wooden floor beneath the kitchen table. The window bench that shone in the most amazing light from their breathtaking backyard displayed an obnoxious number of very loved-looking stuffed animals: an eye missing here, a patched-up arm there. Was that chocolate on another? I didn't touch that one since I wasn't sure.

Beds weren't made and graded homework was sprawled over desks and cabinets, as if it were some type of ivy plant, having a mind of its own and growing faster than a gardener could keep up with and tame.

I couldn't allow myself to just leave it. I washed dishes and cleaned the kitchen. I made the beds and picked up the rooms. I put toys away and tossed dirty clothes into hampers. I may or may not have moved a few things around (I cringe at that). They lived on about an acre, which boasted beautifully manicured lawns surrounded by mature gardens. The day before the family returned home, I'd cut large amounts of wildflowers and roses and lilacs and peonies and others from their backyard, depending on the time of year they vacationed. Finding the cabinet where they kept vases and jars, I'd prepare beautiful arrangements for bedside tables and next to the kitchen sink. The buffet near the entry that now gleamed from my polishing displayed a silver vessel full of small branches from the cherry tree near the playset. Setting freshly baked cookies on the kitchen table, I'd smile.

Letting a breath out as I locked up for the last time before they returned, I thought I'd helped these poor souls who couldn't get a grasp on life now that they had children. *How did they live without me the rest of the year?* I wondered.

Kids are just not my thing, I again convinced myself.

I hate to admit it, but it took years for me to really hear God's voice and release my own expectations of what motherhood looked like and the false reality I had created. A year or so ago I took a class at Denver Seminary. I'm a total nerd, so I was completely geeking out while walking around campus, dreaming of the day when I could actually take courses for credit, not just because I was friends with the professor.

One evening in class we talked about false selves. I'd heard the concept before, but that night the Lord allowed my mind to start churning. Perhaps it was because I had just finished a book called *Confessions of a Raging Perfectionist* by Amanda Jenkins. I know I'm a perfectionist. I get it. I realize it's something to work on. What I didn't realize was that my perfectionism was surrounding me in a false reality of having the ability to control chaos.

Similar to coming up with a completely incorrect view of what life with children looked like, I had an inaccurate view of what life as a follower of Christ resembled. I see now that deep down, I think things were all about me. Christ died for *me*; God has blessed *me* with (fill in the blank); *I* am being used by Him. There were too many I's and me's encased inside my head. The life I have should be less about me and more about being a living example of what God can do.

> *As he passed by, he saw a man blind from birth.*
> *And his disciples asked him, "Rabbi, who sinned, this man*
> *or his parents, that he was born blind?" Jesus answered,*
> *"It was not that this man sinned, or his parents, but that the works*
> *of God might be displayed in him. We must work the works*
> *of him who sent me while it is day; night is coming,*
> *when no one can work. As long as I am in the world,*
> *I am the light of the world." Having said these things, he spit on*
> *the ground and made mud with the saliva. Then he anointed*
> *the man's eyes with the mud and said to him,*
> *"Go, wash in the pool of Siloam" (which means Sent).*
> *So he went and washed and came back seeing.*
> *The neighbors and those who had seen him before as a beggar*
> *were saying, "Is this not the man who used to sit and beg?"*
> *Some said, "It is he." Others said, "No, but he is like him."*
> *He kept saying, "I am the man." So they said to him,*
> *"Then how were your eyes opened?" He answered,*
> *"The man called Jesus made mud and anointed my eyes*
> *and said to me, 'Go to Siloam and wash.'*
> *So I went and washed and received my sight."*
> John 9:1–11 ESV

Did you catch the part where Jesus responded to the question of why the man was blind? He essentially answered, "You're asking the wrong question. This is not the result of sin. Instead of looking for someone to blame, look instead for what God can do. He is blind so the work of God may be put on display."

My incorrect view of children and motherhood had very little to do with me. Instead, like the blind man who could suddenly see, my blindness to the amazing blessing of motherhood is a testament to how God can change someone's story. God knew I'd have children one day and wanted to show a watching world what can happen when someone gives her meticulously arranged life back over to Him.

I lead the women's Bible study at our church, LIFEGATE Denver. Given the opportunity to name our group, we began to refer to ourselves as Pearls + Purpose. Matthew 13:45–46 tells us the kingdom of heaven is valuable like a pearl. Because of this, I started researching what a pearl was and how it was made, and the Lord began revealing to me that life is a bit like a pearl.

Hidden within the walls of a shell, I couldn't see the brilliance of His love until my surroundings (shell) had sprung open. Verve and vitality had been fanned into my world, and I knew God's bigness with more zeal than I ever had before. According to Wikipedia, pearls have become a metaphor for "something rare, fine, admirable, and valuable."[8] I think we all want to be a pearl, but what we don't understand is that it doesn't happen overnight.

Natural pearls, I've learned, begin as a foreign object (such as a parasite or piece of shell) that somehow settles inside an oyster's inner body where it cannot be expelled. Irritated by this intruder, the oyster's body takes defensive action and begins to secrete a smooth calcium carbonate and conchiolin to cover the irritant and protect itself. Over time, layer upon layer, the obstacle is ultimately completely encased by the silky crystalline coating, resulting in the lovely and lustrous gem called a pearl.

How are we not like that pearl? Sure, we are certainly not an irritant to God, but we do have obstacles and concerns and difficulties. Once we're encased in a life with Jesus, though, He will cover us and cover us and cover us some more. Layer upon layer, He will work on our lives and our character, eventually fashioning us into something rare, fine, and valuable.

Matthew 13 tells of Jesus going to sit by the sea. After large crowds began gathering around Him, He got into a boat and sat there looking at the crowd. As the group continued to grow, they stood on the shore, waiting with bated breath for Christ to teach. Using the boat as a pulpit, Jesus began sharing parables, which are stories with a deeper meaning, about the kingdom of heaven.

Or the kingdom of heaven is like a jeweler on the lookout
for the finest pearls. When he found a pearl more beautiful
and valuable than any jewel he had ever seen, the jeweler sold
all he had and bought that pearl, his pearl of great price.
Matthew 13:45–46 VOICE

Christ's story implied that the jeweler was like a person searching for more purpose in life. Something bigger, more valuable. In his searching, he found one pearl of great significance and sold all his possessions to acquire it. So, said Jesus, people seeking a life of abundant blessing who find the gospel (the pearl) should be willing to sacrifice all other things for their newfound treasure. The gospel is being represented in this story as something of far more worth than anything else in life. Jesus's intent was to impress upon our hearts the duty of sacrificing all we are and all we possess in order to obtain the richness of His love.

I knew of this love; in fact, I'd known it since I was five and asked my mom to help "put Jesus into my heart" while we were driving on the freeway in Seattle, Kenny Rogers blasting from the tape deck. That day I learned how to pray and give my heart over to Him. But at that moment I had only just become the speck inside the oyster.

For years upon years, Christ would cover me with His iridescence, growing me layer by layer, knowing my faith would be valuable.

What I didn't understand through the years as I continued to stack filled-up prayer journal after prayer journal onto the shelves next to my bed was that I was meditating on one of my favorite psalms with horrible error. The psalm that I had been focusing on was this:

> *Take delight in the LORD, and he will give you*
> *the desires of your heart.*
> Psalm 37:4 NIV

What I had yet to comprehend was that God doesn't give you the desires of your heart that aren't rooted in Him. The truth of it is, once you position your heart to line up with His, He actually changes your desires. And the funny thing is, He does it so quietly and with such beauty that for a few moments you think your desires are your idea.

God saw fit to prepare Ben and me individually for a time before bringing us together as a couple, knowing exactly who we needed to be for the other person. He also knew we needed to open our hearts in complete abandon to Him and give Him control of our future. Not the future we thought we wanted, but the future He knew was far more fulfilling, stretching, and beautiful than Ben and I ever would have imagined or planned on our own.

Ben and I also saw God weave together our vastly different up-bringings into one amazing story.

Ben's youth is a story of abuse, homelessness, juvenile detention, and a bleak future when he dropped out of high school. Thankfully the Lord doesn't walk away from us at any point in our lives . . . even during salty seasons. Time and time again, hard situations (some brought on by our own actions, others not) will be reused as they turn into something valuable. There are times when God allows something to happen so strength and fortitude of character is birthed, because it will be of great importance and of value at a later point in life.

What do people mean when they say,
"I am not afraid of God because I know He is good"?
Have they never even been to a dentist?
C. S. Lewis

Without the difficult childhood Ben grew up in, he may never have had the opportunity to mature into a man of courage and determination as he became the powerhouse of both grit and moxie that he is today. These are characteristics he'd need in helping our children heal from their pasts of trauma, neglect, and abuse.

My neat and tidy version of childhood wasn't going to cut it when it came to helping heal hearts steeped in grief and pain, for I'd never encountered that type of heartache. Only with our hearts and experiences united, with Christ as our third cord of strength, could we begin sewing back together a child's heart that had been torn in half.

Though one may be overpowered, two can defend themselves.
A cord of three strands is not quickly broken.
Ecclesiastes 4:12 NIV

After traveling the world as a mechanic for the US Cycling team in his late teens and early twenties, Ben pursued his GED while living in Cairo during his father's time in Egypt as the military attaché, finally enrolling in college, where he thrived and graduated with honors.

My sweet husband didn't know anything of God, aside from what he'd picked up on Christmas and Easter services and the random Sunday. Always hating being made to go to church because he "had to act and dress differently than any other day of the week," the concept of a loving, active heavenly Father escaped him. But during his time in university, God revealed Himself to Ben.

Now when he tells his story, Ben views his past differently and can recognize moment after divinely guided moment when the Lord protected or shepherded him through hurts, decisions, and opportunities.

God had already chosen Ben, and though he had certainly allowed some pain to enter his life, the Lord was also continuously protecting him in preparation for the new life he would soon embrace. God's love and laws were being written on Ben's mind and heart long before he ever perceived a change was happening.

> *I will put my laws in their minds*
> *and write them on their hearts.*
> *I will be their God,*
> *and they will be my people.*
> Hebrews 8:10 NIV

Throughout my Bible, I have singled out passages of prayers and encouragement for our kids and my dear husband, penning in their names next to the particular scripture. One of my prayers for Ben is found in Ephesians 1:16–19 (ESV):

> *I do not cease to give thanks for you, remembering you in my prayers, that the God of our Lord Jesus Christ, the Father of glory, may give you the Spirit of wisdom and of revelation in the knowledge of him, having the eyes of your hearts enlightened, that you may know what is the hope to which he has called you, what are the riches of his glorious inheritance in the saints, and what is the immeasurable greatness of his power toward us who believe, according to the working of his great might.*

I just love how The Message translates this passage. I learned long ago that we can place our names into Bible verses to help them feel more personal, and I do this a lot when using Scripture in talking to God. Place the name of a loved one in place of Ben's (below) in these verses from The Message and see how the passage comes alive as we speak life and encouragement into the hearts of others.

Ben, *when I heard of the solid trust you have in the Master Jesus and your outpouring of love to all the followers of Jesus, I couldn't stop thanking God for you—every time I prayed, I'd think of you and give thanks.*

But I do more than thank. Ben, *I ask—ask the God of our Master, Jesus Christ, the God of glory—to make you intelligent and discerning in knowing him personally, your eyes focused and clear, so that you can see exactly what it is he is calling you to do, grasp the immensity of this glorious way of life he has for his followers, oh, the utter extravagance of his work in us who trust him—endless energy, boundless strength!*

It's so exciting and awe-inspiring to know that with Christ, reconciliation and healing are possible. God, You are so supremely good.

> *"Blessed is the one whom God corrects;*
> *so do not despise the discipline of the Almighty.*
> *For he wounds, but he also binds up;*
> *he injures, but his hands also heal."*
> Job 5:17–18 NIV

It's incredible to think that before Ben personally knew who Christ was, God's protective, masterful hand was working to shape him into a pearl. Without Ben's knowledge, our heavenly Father was placing layer upon layer over the wounds in his life, building him into the most incredible man I've ever met—and the perfect other half for me. God continued breaking down walls and barriers through the years as Ben grew in knowledge and love of his heavenly Father.

The Lord was using our unique experiences to embolden each of us to expand our dreams to glorify Him. And to expand our borders.

Now to the God who can do so many awe-inspiring things,
immeasurable things, things greater than we ever could
ask or imagine through the power at work in us,
to Him be all glory in the church and in Jesus the Anointed
from this generation to the next, forever and ever. Amen.
Ephesians 3:20–21 VOICE

There are so many incredible stories within the pages of Scripture of individuals who said *yes* when our heavenly Father asked something of them. It's often hard to remember that these are not simply characters in a book, but actual people who lived and breathed and were scared and passionate and could have taken the comfortable, so-called easy way out. They're really no different from each of us. I mean, sure, they lived in a different time in an entirely different culture. At the core, though, we're the same.

Like us, each of these individuals in our Bibles had to get to a place in their lives where they were okay giving their plans back to God or they weren't fully living. They handed Him their futures and expectations of what life should look like for Him to care for and tend to.

The Bible tells one such story about a woman named Ruth. After her husband died, Ruth's life looked immensely different from what she'd expected it would. But with God's prompting, she followed her mother-in-law into a foreign land and her family line continued. She not only has the honor of being King David's grandmother but is in the lineage of Jesus Christ Himself (Ruth 1–4; Matthew 1:5–6).

Later in the Bible, we read of Esther, who became a queen and had the opportunity to save her people, the Jews, from death. In spite of the valor of her actions, however, she could have been killed herself; but rather than living a life of comfort for the rest of her days, she obeyed the calling her heavenly Father was placing upon her heart. Gaining an extra dose of bravery from her uncle who encouraged her, saying she was "made queen for just such a time as this" (Esther 4:14 NLT), Esther went ahead with God's plans and used her position for furthering God's kingdom and divine purpose.

Esther wasn't the only one born for such a time as this. We could have been born at any time throughout history, so why are we here now? Why did God place you in the country and city and neighborhood you reside in? There is as much purpose in that as there is in our experiences and the lives we've lived.

Whether peppered with pain or jam-packed with joy, Christ will use our experiences for His kingdom . . . if we let Him. Getting to a place where we're ready to let go of our anticipated and carefully structured futures of what life "should" look like doesn't just happen. It takes a deep breath, honest prayer, and faithfully opening our hands in submission to our heavenly Father.

The immense faith it takes to make that first step and to breathe the prayer that God would fully use us in the way He desires is a little bit scary. Actually, it's terrifying . . . and yet somehow we are filled with peace because we trust Him. Exodus 4 shares how Moses told God he wasn't cut out for the job because he wasn't eloquent of speech and tried to shove the task instead onto his brother, Aaron. Moses was also massively overwhelmed by his calling. How did God respond? He basically told Moses, "Who gave you that mouth? Now go. Obey."

God allowed some experiences to burst my love for Him into

a passion. Plans changed; life changed. And by releasing expectations of how I thought life should look, the Lord continued carefully orchestrating change in my heart, molding me into the woman He created me to be.

But now, O LORD, you are our Father;
we are the clay, and you are our potter;
we are all the work of your hand.
Isaiah 64:8 ESV

PART THREE

Uncomfortable

CHAPTER 7

. . . .

Becoming Better, Not Bitter

. . . . . . 🦢 . . . .

Joy isn't found when your situation is perfected.
Joy is experienced when your perspective is shifted. . . .
Circumstances can crush your soul or be a catalyst for joy.
NIRUP ALPHONSE

Thrilled to escape the San Antonio heat for a few days, I flew home to Seattle with the intent of visiting my parents as well as tying up loose ends on the sale of our darling little bungalow we had owned those few short months before our big move. The day after I arrived was warmer than usual, and a dear friend and I took full advantage of the beautiful weather, enjoying crab cakes and muddled strawberry lemonade on the deck of a favorite little spot overlooking Lake Washington. It was a sweet catching up of two friends who have been through so much together, a lifetime of memories in a handful of years. The next morning after an evening absorbed in conversation and laughter, I wasn't feeling well. Praying I hadn't consumed bad crab, a thought of pregnancy rolled through my consciousness.

Convincing myself I was being ridiculous, I spent the next several hours back in bed seesawing in discomfort until I gave in and hopped in the car. Mind swirling with what-ifs, I sped past the neighborhood grocery store that sat next to the Blockbuster Video I had worked at through high school for fear that someone I knew would recognize me and want to chat, and pulled instead into a drugstore parking lot farther from my home. Buying a handful of tests that all spouted promises of being the first to recognize a pregnancy, I rushed back home on autopilot, parking my rental car in the same spot I used to park the rickety old Porsche I'd bought at a garage sale when I was nineteen. I shakily walked back inside my parents' empty house, the silence feeling extremely loud since everyone was at work and I wished they weren't. Joined by Libby, our family dog, I headed to the bathroom (already a sign I'd never have privacy in the bathroom again).

Yep, pregnant. Each test I took said the same thing.

Forgetting that Ben was off hunting with a buddy where reception was nonexistent, I phoned him with a stunned smile on my face. Voice mail. Ruffled, I called my mom, whose assistant shared that she was in a meeting. Well then. Scrolling quickly to my dad's name, I rang him next. Unavailable. Frustration beginning to settle in, I phoned my firefighter brother's phone and my call went straight to voice mail. It was likely his phone was off; he was probably responding to an emergency or catching a quick nap between calls. Mind reeling, I tried my best friend, Kiesha. Negative. I left a hurried message.

Seriously? I thought. *The biggest news ever to hit my uterus and I can't get ahold of a single person?* I had other friends I could call, but I knew all the aforementioned would be seriously hurt I hadn't told them first. Nervous energy poured over me like a tidal wave, so I went for a run.

A loooonnnnggg run.

Over and over and on repeat, an internal conversation flowed through my mind: *I'm pregnant.* (puff puff) *I'm pregnant.* (wait for the crosswalk sign to turn green) *Lord Jesus, are You* serious?!

I. Am. Pregnant.

Instead of a sinking feeling of knowing this was not planned, that we had only been married a handful of months and this wasn't supposed to happen yet, I was surprisingly elated. Well, the scared type of elated. I ran/walked for nearly two hours until I realized I should probably stop before I passed out. I may have worked with women in crisis pregnancy situations, but I suddenly felt like I knew nothing. One thing I did figure though, was that running until I passed out was probably not good for the baby.

Finally making it back home and pressing the brass latch and hobbling through the bright blue door, I bolted upstairs to grab a towel for a much-needed shower. Just then, our elderly Labrador,

Libby, waddled up to me with a frenzied look in her eyes and suddenly collapsed onto the bedroom floor and began seizing!

I stroked her fur and softly spoke to her, making sure she didn't swallow or bite her tongue. I kept thinking of my brother's EMT training and how he'd know how to handle this situation. I phoned him again in a panic. This time he answered both my call as well as my question if this had happened before to Libby. He knew as well as I did that this was a first for our beloved family dog.

Mentally setting aside my big announcement for the rest of the afternoon, I cared only for the dog our family had rescued a decade earlier as she had seizure after seizure in my arms. Eventually I reached my parents, and when they arrived home, we were able to walk through the devastation together, searching for an emergency facility to rush our sweet dog to.

Just before my parents left to take Libby to the animal ER, Kiesha arrived at the door. As I was standing there in the hallway with my family and my best friend, I blurted out, "Um . . . I know this is terrible timing and all, but I found out today that I'm pregnant."

Right then, before anyone could respond, I heard a strange noise coming from upstairs where Libby was resting. Figuring she was seizing yet again, I ran to the stairs, and had just gotten on the first step when she fell down the staircase, flipping and flopping around, with wild, scared eyes looking at me like, *What is going on?! Make this stop!* Oh, sweet Libby. I can hardly type this without letting the tears flow.

She was whisked away to the animal ER, and several hours later my parents came home alone. Libby had a brain tumor and there was nothing they could do. We cried. We sobbed. It was a rough day in the Swanstrom household.

Thankfully, we had another life to be excited about and help us grieve the loss of our wonderful family member. Not the best way or day to find out you were about to start the next limb in your family tree, but God knew we needed a little joy on that dark day. By the way, I finally got ahold of Ben to share the news that he was going to be a dad. I honestly don't remember much of our conversation, but I do remember the excitement and wonder in our voices.

Back in San Antonio, Ben and I were finally in our new house (sans the bachelor roommates) and I was able to wrap my mind around the fact that I was becoming a mom. Laughing that I used to think I never wanted children, I was thrilled to start planning. My pregnancy may have been a total surprise, but as soon as it sank in, I took control of it and everything was thought out with intention. I had all the apps and frequented all the websites, making sure I knew what to expect as I was expecting. I gobbled up book after book and had very strong feelings about *Baby Wise*, breast-feeding, cloth diapers, and homemade baby food. I parented really well, while that little baby was in my womb. I decided I'd be a great and successful mom if I'd just stick to the instruction manuals.

Each doctor's appointment confirmed we were taking one step away from our newlywed adventure and stepping closer toward a family of three. We were eager to learn the sex of the little one growing inside me, but when the doctor shared it was a boy, I don't think I was adequately prepared for the news. I was still absorbing all the changes we would undergo with a newborn, but now this newborn was becoming a little person—my baby boy. I was in awe of knowing that this boy I carried inside me already had an entire life planned out by our Creator. As Ben and I prayed over our baby boy, we were excited for all the adventures God has in store for him. We decided to go with an African safari theme for his bedroom, and I splurged on the perfect zebra-striped rug from Pottery Barn and hung a wall full of breathtaking black-and-white photography of dusty elephants, giraffes stretching their necks to reach the top of the tree leaves, and lions snuggling their young. Motherhood was easy, I decided, and I had it all figured out, down to the darling pre-Pinterest decorated nursery.

All of a sudden though, things came to a screeching halt. My tides of feeling poorly suddenly turned into debilitating nausea and I began to throw up every twenty minutes. When I was at work, I ignored it as best I could, sweat trickling down my temples as I swallowed down the nausea for fear these women with unplanned pregnancies would go running for the door. I closed my eyes tightly and visualized sitting in a session and saying, "Pregnancy is such a blessing. Really! Oh, excuse me for a moment." Cue my run for the bathroom.

Sigh . . . it was awesome.

I christened Target parking lots, wastebaskets, and it's taken me over a decade to eat at Chipotle again (you don't want to know). Ben would come home from work to find me passed out in the hallway of our home, having attempted to grab a glass of water in the kitchen. Other days my poor husband would find our chocolate lab, Thatcher, curled up next to me as I hugged the toilet bowl after falling asleep exhausted from heaving. Needless to say, it was rough. Worse than rough. My eyes would zero in on restroom signs, the closest wastebaskets, or even the nearest exits to parking lots or grass. Every moment of every day, I felt like I needed to find the nearest place to, well, you know.

My doctor, whom I absolutely cherish, became a dear friend through my constant visits to her office and was my biggest supporter. Her nurses all knew to patch me through immediately when I called, and by the end I even had her personal cell phone number. Constantly on massive amounts of medication typically used to keep chemotherapy patients' nausea at bay, I can't even put into words how awful I still felt. I was secretly jealous of those cute pregnant girls who glowed and loved being "with child." I was just not that girl, and sometimes fought with despair over it.

I worked as long as I could, but my constant vomiting made it difficult to concentrate on the girls and women who needed the best of me when they came for counsel. Finally I couldn't ignore it any longer, and it was time for me to step away from working with these women who held my heart so tightly and focus on my own coming child. I continued coming in often, bringing in my own clothes that I quickly outgrew. Though I felt the Lord releasing me of my time there, I hoped even something as little as a new maternity shirt, shorts, or jeans would bring the women a tiny bit of joy, knowing they were loved and God truly cared about them and what happened to their babies.

...🦢...

In the past, I've shared that my morning sickness took away some of the joy in my pregnancy, but I actually don't think that's true. It may have removed some of the pregnancy bliss as my baby boy grew in my womb, but I fought intensely to keep my joy. When I was in high school our youth pastor asked once what we'd like to have more than anything else. My response was that I wanted to find joy in all situations. I've paid deep deference to the concept of joy since then.

> Joy cannot be dictated by circumstance; instead, we need to allow it to be linked to promises that have been laid out before us throughout Scripture.

Joy isn't meant to be a by-product of a perfect or easy life; it instead shows the heart's position during struggle. The reality is that my health or the way I feel emotionally cannot correspond to my joy because as my dear friend and pastor Nirup Alphonse says, "The joy we experience is a direct result of the perspective we have of Christ Jesus."[9] It's easy to have joy when life is rainbows and unicorns, but the instant something goes awry and away from perfectly laid out plans, will we drop joy into a pile of rubble, with the mind-set that it's too difficult to hold on to when life goes for the jugular? Joy cannot be dictated by circumstance; instead, we need to allow it to be linked to promises that have been laid out before us throughout Scripture.

I pray that God, the source of all hope,
will infuse your lives with an abundance of joy and peace
in the midst of your faith so that your hope will overflow
through the power of the Holy Spirit.
Romans 15:13 VOICE

Paul, who wrote much of the New Testament, says this in 2 Corinthians 11:23–27 (MSG):

I've worked much harder, been jailed more often, beaten up more times than I can count, and at death's door time after time. I've been flogged five times with the Jews' thirty-nine lashes, beaten by Roman rods three times, pummeled with rocks once. I've been shipwrecked three times, and immersed in the open sea for a night and a day. In hard traveling year in and year out, I've had to ford rivers, fend off robbers, struggle with friends, struggle with foes. I've been at risk in the city, at risk in the country, endangered by desert sun and sea storm, and betrayed by those I thought were my brothers. I've known drudgery and hard labor, many a long and lonely night without sleep, many a missed meal, blasted by the cold, naked to the weather.

And yet, with this as part of his story, Paul shared about the joy he had in Christ. I might not be flogged or shipwrecked. Even so, struggles, however they look in that particular season, can still attempt to overtake delighting in the Lord. Having the opposite of an easy pregnancy, where my body was debilitated and unwell for months on end, actually causing me to lose weight rather than gaining it, could have racked me with a discouraged pessimism. But though I certainly had moments of despair, I knew that God saw me in my brokenness, just like He always has.

The reality is that no one can steal our joy; it's something that we have to choose to hand over and release from our grasp. We must refuse to let circumstances make us bitter, but pray they instead make us better. Jesus bought and paid for my freedom and yours, and joy rests in that gift of salvation. However, I still struggle, and maybe you do too. I wrestle with wondering why all I focus on is my lack of joy when life isn't flawless, but don't recognize overwhelming joy when life is going grand.

Paul later says in 2 Corinthians 12:7–9 (MSG):

> *Satan's angel did his best to get me down; what he in fact did was push me to my knees. No danger then of walking around high and mighty! At first I didn't think of it as a gift, and begged God to remove it. Three times I did that, and then he told me,*
>
> *My grace is enough; it's all you need.*
> *My strength comes into its own in your weakness.*

Our beautiful, precious, baby boy finally arrived on April 17 . . . exactly ten days late, even after being induced. After finding out we were having a boy, we scoured baby name books, looked through family albums, and prayed for inspiration, but nothing was standing out. But now this baby was here and he needed a name—and he couldn't leave the hospital without one! My doctor sat with us for over half an hour brainstorming names. Finally we decided on Anton, a shortened version of Antony, my dad's middle name. Ben also felt a connection to the name Anton because of a close college friend who had tragically drowned. So, with deep affection for my father and for the young life that ended too soon, Anton Christian Anderson came home with both a name and a legacy. The week he was born was the same week my brother moved in with us because he didn't want his nephew growing up with him on the other side of the country. I don't remember if he knew the guest room was across the hall from the nursery, but I do remember laughing while buying him earplugs.

I realized pretty quickly after the nausea set in that my pregnancy was not going as planned, but when Anton arrived, all my great parenting also went out the window. Just like I had planned out my life years before, I had gotten caught up in taking control of the details once again.

When will I learn? I wondered.

Embracing the fact that I thought I knew everything from reading all the books, blogs, and websites, and actually knowing nothing because I had no life experience with actual human babies, I had moments of pure panic and others of genuine giddiness that he was mine. I'd never felt love like this before. Parents always said it, but I couldn't comprehend the feeling until I held that little floppy-headed baby in my arms. I thought I loved chocolate and flowers and Italy. But those loves didn't hold a candle to this new kind of love— the love a mother has for her child.

> We must refuse to let circumstances make us bitter, but pray they instead make us better.

I would do anything for my son. I would give up sleep and hot meals. I would rock him for fifty hours straight if that meant he was happy and healthy. I would go to the ends of the earth to ensure his well-being and that he felt loved and was taken care of in the best and fullest way possible. He could never do anything that would stop me from loving him.

For the first time in my life, I began to understand all the Bible references to God the Father and how He must feel about me. I'd heard the verses before; I had studied the passages. But that was all head knowledge, and now I had heart knowledge, too. The cliché-sounding conversations we'd had in Sunday school and youth group were right: Jesus loves me so much that He left the paradise of heaven to walk around on earth for thirty-three years, knowing He would pay the ultimate price and die for me. I'd known this for years, but it suddenly felt specific, not generalized in the fact that He had sacrificed Himself for all of us, but that He'd done so for me personally (go to page 256 for more).

God, the Creator of the entire universe, knows my name and loves me deeply. That notion washed over me anew as I peered down at my wrinkly baby who was so perfectly part me and part Ben. Becoming a mother, I now had a pinprick of understanding God's heart. I would willingly give up my life for my child if it meant saving him. I marveled at the self-sacrificial magnitude of this love.

A few short months after little Anton was born, we were surprised with double lines showing up on yet another pregnancy test, throwing us into a new life as parents of two little children just over a year apart. Despite this second pregnancy also being a challenge, I still loved being pregnant because I chose to find joy in it as I honed in on the little delights and knew when our second baby was in my arms, the magnitude of my struggle would feel so worth it. I suppose it's one of those times when there is a large difference between like and love. I didn't like it, but I did love it so very much. Having a baby truly is a miracle, especially once I could feel the little one wiggling around in my womb—the sweetest gift of all. In those last weeks, when I marveled how my skin could stretch any tighter to allow for the little one to grow inside my swollen belly, I would stare at the black-and-white photograph of that young boy in Malawi that we won at the auction years earlier. Knowing that picture was the catalyst that first put the idea of adoption into our minds, I wondered if I could love an adopted child as much as I loved the children from my own womb, and if we really had the courage to obey God and go for it.

Two days before my due date with our second baby boy, I called my doctor on her cell phone. With tears streaming down my cheeks, I told her to "get this baby out of me. Now." I simply couldn't be pregnant any longer. I was in so much pain and was so tired of throwing up so many times a day. Reminding her that I'd been pregnant for nearly two years straight, she chuckled knowingly, and scheduled me to be induced the next morning. After being in the hospital over twenty-four hours, I was sent home with the nurses shrugging that it didn't take.

Little Laith Rutger Anderson finally arrived the next day, blue as a Smurf after an emergency C-section. I guess the way he entered the world was simply foreshadowing all the times we'd be in the hospital with him. Since he learned to walk, we've called him Crazy Crash. He's been the first one of our boys to break a bone and have surgery, and he has had a slew of health issues. He says the hospital is his "happy place." He is named after two of our favorite men in the world, our friend Laith Anderson, whom we now call "Big Laith," and my brother, Erik Rutger. Both of these men are as strong as they are tender. We wanted our son to know that you can be both tough and compassionate, that those characteristics are not exclusive. And from the day we brought him home from the hospital, and even every visit since, he's been our tenderhearted one who wants to become a pediatric brain or heart surgeon one day. He would (and has) give the shirt off his back. He never has money in his pocket because he spends it on other people before he's able to use it on himself. We knew, even early on that these two boys of ours were going to become great brothers someday.

After Laith was born, I'd barely begun to figure out how to live life with two babies, take a shower every day, and serve something for dinner other than cereal or grilled cheese, and yet it was undeniable that God was whispering to Ben and me. Reminding us of our desire to live a life outside ourselves, the Lord urged us to expand our family again. This time He wasn't going to make the decision for us, placing a baby in my womb. This new (and slightly scary) way required obedience and a willingness to act. With wide eyes and open hearts, we began researching adoption.

CHAPTER 8

* * * * * * * * * * * * * *

Free-falling

* * * * * * 🦢 * * * * * *

Falling into the will of God
takes guts and grit we don't have.
Of course we're nervous.
We can't handle this alone.
And that's precisely the point.

SHANNAN MARTIN

When I was young I spent a short season as a Camp Fire Girl. Like Girl Scouts, we earned badges and did all sorts of volunteer work and community service in hopes of growing into women who led well and cared about the community around us. One project, though, felt confusing to me as a young girl, with emotions swirling around my heart that I had never faced before. We were to plant a tree in honor of someone we went to school with who had recently died in a fire.

This sweet elementary-age girl had lived in an apartment near our neighborhood grocery store. Because it was on a busy street in an area we frequented, we passed the building often. I remember seeing the charred, blackened section a few floors up—the place that was supposed to give her shelter and safety ended up being a place of destruction and bereavement because she couldn't jump.

I think of her often, that little girl. I don't remember her name or what grade she had been in, but I like to think that even though her life was cut short, it had significant purpose. Why? Because she reminds me daily that I cannot live in fear. There are times when I need to jump.

There are times when challenges and dreams and great purposes require us to leap in order to realize them, just as you must leap from the window to escape a burning building. You *have* to. But you are scared and you are standing on the windowsill, tightly gripping its sides. Your feet feel glued to the wooden frame beneath you. You're afraid the leap might be more of a fall, landing right on your face. You're more fearful of what *might* happen when you let go and step into the unknown than the inevitable if you don't.

And then you realize the time has come. There's no turning back. You either jump, or you don't. There is no option for both or neither; you must choose one.

Years later, when adoption was clearly something God was laying on my heart and Ben's, we knew our decision needed to be evidenced in action. We knew that even though jumping felt scary, we were confident it was necessary and purposeful. So we made our choice—we released our grip of the windowsill and . . . just . . . jumped.

After years of growing in our relationship with Christ independently and then as a unified couple, and after deep down knowing Ben and I would adopt, God whispered to our hearts, *It's time.* All the years leading to this very moment He was patiently preparing us. We were completely and utterly thrilled. And also completely and utterly terrified.

We knew we wanted to adopt from Africa; that part was never in question. But then we began to research what countries were open and which we qualified for. Countries open for adoption have differing regulations on who can adopt: how long you've been married, how old you are, and how many other children you have, among other qualifications. After initially daydreaming about bringing in children from many places around the globe, having a sort of United Nations within the walls of our home, we laughed at the absurdity of having so many kids (sweet, sweet irony).

Instead, we decided we'd immerse ourselves and pour into one country and culture. Feeling incapable to do this well in the rare chance we brought home more than one child, we desired to make provisions and plan for the what-ifs. We wanted to dig deep and shunned the idea of bringing a child home and washing their birth country off them. It was important to us that we teach all our children about the holidays and history, the food and people of the country we would be forever tied to. As we learned more and more about each country, Ben and I fell head over heels for Ethiopia. Without a doubt, this was the country God was leading us to.

And thus commenced the craziness.

After what seemed like thousands of hours of working on it, we submitted our paperwork in the spring and learned new things about ourselves within that process. One form in particular asked what we would and would not accept in a referral (child).

Were we okay with skin discoloration? How about a cleft lip? What about a missing finger, hand, or limb? Or what about blindness, or a child who is deaf? It covered *everything* you could ever think of and about a million things you never have.

Ben and I deeply struggled over those pages. Each description was a child. A real child who was waiting for a family. Each *no* felt like saying, "Nope. we don't want you, we want someone else." Oh, how we agonized over that list. We prayed and prayed over each and every *yes* and *no* that we checked. Yes, we'd accept minor health issues; no, we weren't prepared for severe special needs.

The big thing we kept coming back to was that we would love and cherish that child with special needs, whether they had a blood disease, were autistic, or had Down syndrome. Of course we would. But it would likely prevent us from adopting any more children because we'd want to make sure we were taking the necessary time and dedication for surgeries, therapy, and general loving-on-by-mom-and-dad time while still being a good mom and dad for our biological boys.

We poured over and prayed through this agonizing list, feeling as if our very hearts were being audited. But our heavenly Father used every conversation that flowed from the difficult questions as the beginning of a continued calling. With it came a spark, an idea. From it grew a desire as God prepared us to adopt more than this one child.

After all our i's were dotted and t's were crossed, on to the infant waiting list we went. The days turned into weeks and the weeks turned into months and my heart began to ache. Really, really ache.

Some callings have a start date that we can see, that we can manage and assess. Like pregnancy, for example. A woman knows she'll be pregnant for fortyish weeks and then—*Boom!* Her life changes forever and she becomes a woman whose heart walks around outside her body. The same is true with going to college and various other things where we can prepare for certain seasons to change.

The planner in all of us loves the ability to see the light at the end of the tunnel, and we desire to view it with such clarity and detail that we could make a paper chain, like a kindergartener would in preparation for Christmas to begin. Who wouldn't like to rip a construction-paper link off each day as a countdown? Better believe I'm raising my hand here.

Oftentimes, though, we're in a huge valley called Wait. We have no idea when our season will change or if our calling will come to fruition.

We made that initial jump only to wait. And wait. Then wait some more.

And that's when it got hard.

So what do we do in this time of wait? How do we trust God knows what He's doing when it kind of feels as if He's forgotten all about us?

All through the Bible God gives us examples of His goodness and perfect timing. He doesn't step away for a moment, nor is He too busy helping someone else. His omnipresence ensures that He is with us during every moment of every day; in fact, He even promises it in Matthew 28:20 (ESV), saying, "I am with you always, to the end of the age."

Not "I'm with you sometimes," "I'm with you most of the time," or "I'm with you when I'm not busy doing other things." He's with us *always*. Every single moment of good, bad, ugly, and in the mundane waiting period.

Here's the thing, though: God uses these waiting times because we have something to learn from them.

During this time, I clung to Hannah's story found in 1 Samuel. She struggled with infertility for years. So long, in fact, that her husband, who loved her dearly, felt the need to marry a second wife in order to continue his family line. In biblical times, a life of infertility was a devastation. Not just emotionally like it is today, but it bore deep shame and even put the husband and wife's future at risk because without children to care for them, they would likely be forced into destitution as they grew older.

Every year Hannah, her husband, and his other wife, Peninnah, would travel to Shiloh and give their yearly sacrifice to the Lord for Passover. And every year at that temple Hannah would be overcome with grief as she poured her heart out to God, telling Him that if He gave her a child, she would give back her child to Him in thanks for His goodness.

This happened year after year after year.

It's significant that we learn that "she continued praying before the LORD" (1 Samuel 1:12 ESV). This wasn't a quick little prayer she shot up while doing the dishes or while sitting in traffic. This was a repeated request bathed in hot tears. There was probably ugly crying going on much of the time she prayed about it. Year after year she laid her request at His feet, and she did it while living authentically.

It's okay to be upset or angry. God understands that valleys and plains are often difficult seasons to live in, especially when we don't know how long the season will last. He can handle our grief and frustration just as He handled Hannah's. God isn't spiteful; He doesn't become enraged when we tell Him we're struggling with a season we're in or something we're experiencing. Our God is a kind, loving, and patient God. If your child came to you saying he was wrestling and having a difficult time with a decision you made that affected his life, how would you react? Would your face turn red and eyes burn in fury? Of course not! You would sit and listen as your beloved child poured his heart out, and though his words may not change the outcome, you'd remind him how much you love and adore him, and assure him that there is purpose behind every decision you make. The same is with God.

Perhaps you have an unfulfilled dream, something you've been praying years for that just hasn't come to pass. Something deep down in your soul that has yet to happen and it's crushing you so fully that like Hannah, so desperate for a child, there are times you can't even eat (1 Samuel 1:7). Your heart is so heavy that there are times you can hardly handle life.

That's the season Hannah was in within the beginning pages of 1 Samuel. It's where she lived for longer than she'd like to admit and it was tearing her apart. And yet she never gave up hope. She never lost faith that God is good.

When we cannot see God's timetable, that is when faith steps in. Do we have faith enough to believe He is actually doing things behind the scenes? How much waiting is too much? When is too long? A month? A year? A decade?

It's like praying at mile marker one and lifting up our request at each mile, not realizing at mile marker 103 He's going to fulfill our request. We're ready. Our heart and character are ready. The circumstances of it all are in alignment with His will.

But what if we give up at mile marker 102? What then? Will we think God is not good because He didn't give us what our heart was exploding over?

Never give up praying. But we also must never give up our time in God's Word, the Bible. Just today I was scrolling through Instagram and came upon a beautiful reminder from one of my favorite Bible Divers (men and women who deeply study the Bible), Beth Moore. She said, "You and I can't fulfill our calling without being in the Scriptures."[10]

Hannah prayed and bared her heart to the Lord at the temple.

She didn't have access to the Scriptures like we do today, so she went to the place where she knew she could find Him, and yet God had heard her every year whether in the temple or at home. He had been by her side during every tear shed. And finally, when the timing was in alignment with His will, the prophet Eli confirmed her dream was coming true. The Lord had blessed the immovability of her faith and ended her season of wait as He opened her womb.

But what happens if we let go of the windowsill and rather than free-falling to safety, we feel like the firefighters who are holding the big round pillow/trampoline, like in a black-and-white movie, will miss us and we land flat on our faces?

What about that girl from your Bible study group who has been on the waiting list to adopt for five years, only to get word that the country they have been trying to adopt from has nearly closed its doors on international adoptions?

What about the family in your neighborhood who moved across the country and bought a new house only to find the husband laid off a few months later?

What about a friend who moved to Uganda for a ministry that suddenly closed its doors?

What about my uncle who, after having a seizure while driving on the freeway, discovered not only that he has brain cancer but that without a miracle sent straight from heaven, he will live only one to two more years? He and my aunt have eleven children (mostly adopted through foster care) and currently have two still in the home.

All this seems unfair. Devastatingly unfair.

Don't get me wrong, I think God is good and faithful . . . but there are certainly times where it doesn't feel like He is, since we only see the falling part and not the position we will be in when we land.

Jeremiah 29:11 (ESV) says, "For I know the plans I have for you, declares the LORD, plans for welfare and not for evil, to give you a future and a hope." This is a popular verse. It is quoted frequently. It's written on coffee mugs, canvases, and sports gear. It's highlighted three times over in my own Bible. We think we're being good Christians when we have it memorized and use it to encourage people around us when they're in a rough or confusing season.

But here's the thing . . . it doesn't mean what we think it means.

We often forget that though the Bible is *for* us, it's not *about* us. God didn't ask the prophet Jeremiah to place that verse in the Bible to help you feel better after your date with that guy from your apartment building goes south or the job you were perfect for didn't pan out.

When read in context, we see this passage isn't written to those of us cozily sitting in Starbucks with an iced two-pump nonfat caramel macchiato in our hands, but rather to the wounded hearts of the Israelites who lived in captivity in Babylon. God was with His people and had a plan—yes, of course He was and He did—but at the same time, God allowed the Jews to be conquered and forced into exile.

If you think about it, this means that God allowed His people to be taken away from their land and their homes. No longer were they able to worship at the temple, which was at the center of their religion and culture. Instead, the Israelites became aliens in Babylon, whose king demanded they worship the Babylonians' god or be burned alive.

When we open our Bibles and leaf back a chapter, reading Jeremiah 28 and the entirety of 29, we'll learn some very important details: God's people disobeyed Him in every possible way. They exchanged Him for evil gods and chose cannibalism and the worship of demons over bowing to the One True God. As a direct result of that disobedience, God allowed them to be forced into exile, marching them eight hundred miles away from home and into a pagan land.

Jeremiah and a false prophet (someone who claims to hear from God, but is a deceiver and spreads lies) named Hananiah were in conversation when Hananiah made a bold statement: God would restore Israel within two years. He would restore their land, their possessions, their livelihood, and the tens of thousands of Israelites forced into slavery would be brought home . . . all within this two-year timetable.

Jeremiah responded to the man with discernment, saying, "Amen! May the LORD do so! May the LORD fulfill the words you have prophesied," (Jeremiah 28:6 NIV) and as the Lord continued to reveal the truth to Jeremiah, Jeremiah confronted the false prophet with a message from God Himself: "Listen, Hananiah, the LORD has not sent you, and you have made this people trust in a lie" (Jeremiah 28:15 ESV).

Entering into chapter 29, Jeremiah further shares God's heart with His people:

> *"Build houses and make yourselves at home.*
>
> *"Put in gardens and eat what grows in that country.*
>
> *"Marry and have children. Encourage your children to marry and have children so that you'll thrive in that country and not waste away.*
>
> *"Make yourselves at home there and work for the country's welfare.*
>
> *"Pray for Babylon's well-being. If things go well for Babylon, things will go well for you."*
>
> Jeremiah 29:5–7 MSG

Essentially what he was saying is, "Thrive there and pray for those around you."

Today we're bombarded with our current version of Hananiah telling us the same thing: life will work out; all will be well. Prosperity and success are coming; we just need to claim our victory. We recite our watered-down version of Jeremiah 29:11 and desire joy, though we want it without having to go into exile to receive it. We want a relationship with Christ, but we aren't willing to take the time out of our busy schedules to be with Him. We choose things over God, just as the Israelites did all those years ago.

What we must remember is that how we handle hardship and interruptions will impact our future. We need to recognize what determines our joy. God allows things to happen so we can learn from them, and even in those hard seasons, His desire is that we thrive. Free-falling may not always feel free, but rather disorderly and turbulent, and yet He patiently and calmly waits to catch us.

The true explanation of this passage is that God most certainly had a plan and it would be carried out, though it would not look anything like the Israelites thought it should. Their pain meant something. As they learned to thrive, God would fully restore and reestablish them.

We form a depth and confidence of trust in our heavenly Father when we are forced to cling to Him through pain. As our need for Him intensifies, He promises to bring us out of the pain and confusion, establishing a future for us.

> *You will seek me and find me, when you seek me*
> *with all your heart. I will be found by you,*
> *declares the LORD, and I will restore your fortunes*
> *and gather you from all the nations and all the places where*
> *I have driven you, declares the LORD, and I will bring you*
> *back to the place from which I sent you into exile.*
> Jeremiah 29:13–14 ESV

Finally, after what felt like forever, we got an e-mail from the director of our agency. The e-mail was filled with a medical report and a dozen photos of an adorable one-year-old little boy. We were next in line for a child, and the e-mail asked if we were interested in accepting his referral. *Is this HIM? Is this our son?* I thought to myself as Ben and I scrolled through the photos. He was on the upper end of the age we were hoping for, and though our boys are so crazy fun, I was yearning for a daughter.

We prayed over this baby boy, we prayed for our family, we prayed for wisdom, and we didn't feel like he was ours.

Ben called the director of our agency and asked if she knew who was next in line if we didn't accept his referral. She assured Ben that the family after us was amazing and lovely. "And," she said, "they have been praying for a one-year-old baby boy."

With this joy-filled confirmation and knowledge that our *no* meant another family would be reaping the blessing of answered prayers, we felt confident in our decision to hand the referral over to this loving and waiting family.

As the seasons changed with the newness that parenthood brings, we pushed away feelings of stagnation and remained in a time of wait, falling into His arms as we decided to thrive in the interim.

Then, one morning in August, giddy to be on vacation in San Diego with Ben's family, I tied my shoes in preparation for a run on my favorite beach with my dear friend Andrea. Looking forward to hearing the sound of the surf crashing onto the sand as we half-jogged, half-conversed deeply about life, I glanced at my e-mail before heading out the door.

Heart pounding wildly, I recognized our director's name in my in-box. Calling Ben to come in from the other room, we opened it to find the e-mail was introducing us to a baby girl. My breath was stolen from within me as we once again scrolled through a multitude of photos and read the medical report (miniscule though it was) for this tiny baby who was only a couple weeks old.

I knew the moment I saw the first grainy photo that she was our daughter.

That run on the beach became one of the sweetest moments of my life as Andrea and I giggled and laughed and screamed the whole way down the boardwalk and back. Then the realization came that we had more waiting to do. I felt God's comfort as my thoughts drifted back to when we first felt Him prompting us toward adoption, toward the calling He was placing upon our lives.

Once again, there was preparation in the wait. I prayed I'd have the patience to wait well since I acknowledged the fact that just because we now had a baby we were pursuing, it didn't mean we got to jump on the next Ethiopia Airlines flight and bring her home. Months and months of waiting ensued as paperwork was submitted in this beautiful (yet very slooooow) third-world country.

Through our excitement, we were very conscious of a dark shadow looming over the calendar. In October, Ethiopia's government shuts down for their rainy season. In fact, people kept telling us that basically the whole country shuts down as torrential rain falls every day and overwhelms the roads, the homes built of tarps and corrugated metal, and the markets shaded by thin woven fabric. The capital, Addis Ababa, has many paved streets and highways, but even in this big, thriving city there are many dirt or cobblestone roads that become a big stretch of muck and make traveling and living (more) difficult.

We knew that if paperwork didn't clear before the date in October, we would have to wait many additional months to first visit, then bring home our daughter. During this time praying without ceasing took on a whole new meaning for me. We prayed fervently and jumped once again while fiercely trusting that God would catch us in His strong arms.

Rejoice always, pray without ceasing,
give thanks in all circumstances;
for this is the will of God in Christ Jesus for you.
1 Thessalonians 5:16–18 ESV

CHAPTER 9

Praying for the Desire to Pray

*We never know how God will answer our prayers,
but we can expect that He will get us involved in His plan
for the answer. If we are true intercessors,
we must be ready to take part in God's work
on behalf of the people for whom we pray.*

CORRIE TEN BOOM

At that point we knew when the country would shut down (it's slightly different every year, depending on when the rains come), and I fervently prayed the specifics and deep desires I had for our daughter and for our expanding family. I prayed before my feet hit the ground in the morning, as I made my coffee, and as I did laundry. I spoke to God while playing with Anton and Laith, during my errand running, as we thanked Him for our blessings during dinner, and of course as I crawled into bed.

For the first time in my life, prayer consumed me.

I wasn't just praying; I was living in expectation that He was looking into my heart and that He heard my requests.

> *In the morning, LORD, you hear my voice;*
> *in the morning I lay my requests before you*
> *and wait expectantly.*
> Psalm 5:3 NIV

> *Evening, morning and noon*
> *I cry out in distress,*
> *and he hears my voice.*
> Psalm 55:17 NIV

August bled into September, and as fall ripened, we found ourselves in October without any news or update. As days and weeks flew by, knowing my October birthday was quickly coming into view, it seemed to be less and less likely she would be coming home with us this year. But I didn't give up. Clinging boldly to the words in Matthew 17:20, I kept thinking of the mustard seed.

*Because you have so little faith. I tell you this: if you had even
a faint spark of faith, even faith as tiny as a mustard seed, you
could say to this mountain, "Move from here to there," and because of your faith, the mountain would move. If you had just a
sliver of faith, you would find nothing impossible.*
Matthew 17:20 VOICE

Faith even as small as a mustard seed could move a mountain!
Instead of admitting defeat, I gathered up every shred of confidence I
had and poured my heart out to God.

*And the Lord said, "Listen to what the unjust judge says.
And will not God bring about justice for his chosen ones,
who cry out to him day and night? Will he keep putting them off?
I tell you, he will see that they get justice, and quickly.
However, when the Son of Man comes,
will he find faith on the earth?*
Luke 18:6–8 NIV

Perhaps God thought I was a bit of a squeaky wheel. But He also
knew my heart and knew how badly I wanted this both for myself and
for our daughter. In it, though, I made sure He knew I wasn't gripping it. I wasn't holding my wish and prayer so tightly that I'd come
completely unglued if He didn't answer it in the way I wanted. This
was *His* little girl, and He knew what was best for her, for me, for Ben,
and for our little boys, who would soon have a baby sister.

I pretended I was a modern-day character in the persistent widow
allegory from Luke 18, which illustrates the important lesson of praying without ceasing.

*Then Jesus told his disciples a parable to show them that they
should always pray and not give up. He said: "In a certain town
there was a judge who neither feared God nor cared what people*

thought. And there was a widow in that town who kept coming to him with the plea, 'Grant me justice against my adversary.'

"*For some time he refused. But finally he said to himself, 'Even though I don't fear God or care what people think, yet because this widow keeps bothering me, I will see that she gets justice, so that she won't eventually come and attack me!'"*

Luke 18:1–5 NIV

I understand that sometimes God doesn't answer in the way we desire. There are moments we petition Him with everything in our being, even to the very depths of our souls, and He is silent. Or He gives a *no*. I don't know why some requests are answered and some are not.

I don't know why my uncle has been given such a short time frame of life when both of his parents are in their nineties. Though they are alive, their minds are lost and confused. Maybe the Lord will provide a miracle, or maybe God is protecting him from the loss of his mind when he grows old. None of us, especially his wife and children, are ready to lose him, none of us will give up praying daily for a miracle, but perhaps the Lord is ready for him to be home in heaven so he can welcome each of us into the gates of eternity when we walk through them.

Maybe he's just the lucky one who gets there first.

None of these thoughts mean for one second that we should put the brakes on how often or how intensely we approach God's throne. It is with confidence and the belief that He will give us all we ask that we continue with a spirit of tenacity. Because nothing is impossible for Him. Absolutely nothing.

During the months it took for us to bring home our baby girl, we pondered and prayed and searched for the perfect name for her. She had a name already, of course, but no one knew who had given it to her, so it held no real significance. We wanted something that held the beauty of her Ethiopian heritage without being difficult to say or spell. After weeks and months of scouring Ethiopian history and reading baby-name book after baby-name book, my eyes fell on the name Imani, meaning "faith." So many hopes and fears and aspirations for our tiny daughter were wrapped up perfectly with the assurance of faith as the cornerstone.

When the wait felt too long and too much to bear, I started a journal for her. Part conversation, part pouring my heart out, I wrote letters to her and prayers that I wanted blanketed over her: things like prayers of protection, health, speed of process, and that she was being loved on. On my birthday I wrote this:

October 29, 2010

Imani,

I am sitting at my gate at the airport . . . headed to meet you! I am completely freaking out and haven't been able to sleep in days.

And today is my birthday! This is the best birthday gift in the entire world. Lord Jesus, You are so gracious!

I have been praying for months and months that I would get to be with you on my birthday and that you would be home by Christmas. Both were completely ridiculous prayers because of the timeline they were giving us. But I prayed it anyway! And I prayed in confidence.

I heard a devotional recently from Proverbs 31 Ministries that talked about praying confidently and specifically. I feel like I always ask God for something and then follow up with "if it's in Your will, Lord" or "if that's okay." And of course I want His will, but it's also okay to really want and desire something . . .

. . . Anyway, I figured hey, it's kind of unrealistic to my human mind, but what's time to God? He invented time, He can do what He wants with it.

And then we got the call! The director of our agency said

that if all goes smoothly and we pass court the first time, we could potentially have you home in the middle of December!

Unreal. Completely unreal.

God, You are so good! You really do listen to our prayers.

By the grace of God, Imani did come home before Christmas. In fact, we took our second trip to Ethiopia and brought her home mere days after Thanksgiving.

...🦢...

Though I've been praying since before I could tie my own shoes, it hasn't always felt comfortable. Sometimes I've felt like my words were raised up but fell flat, and I realize now there have even been times when I prayed more for ritual than actual belief that it would change anything. Thankfully, God knows I'm a work in progress.

Those endless-feeling months of waiting to bring Imani home were the first time I prayed fervently. It was the first glimpse of what I think the Lord was asking me to learn many years ago when one of my closest friends in college was heading to India during spring break. She asked me to be her "prayer warrior." This was the first time my heart had ever stirred by the idea of being a "prayer warrior," and I felt as if God was whispering to me that this was His desire for me, that He wanted me to learn what this meant and begin to live it. I had every intention of approaching the throne throughout the days she was gone, I really did. I wanted to pour out my heart and petition the Lord to protect her and her team as they did big things in His name. Except I was at a total loss on how, what, and when to pray for her. I felt like a total failure. Instead, I simply prayed for her here and there when it occurred to me that I probably should do so.

I knew it should be more; I even wanted it to be more . . . yet during those days, praying was something I did at bedtime when I wrote in my prayer journal and very infrequently in the midst of my day. If someone brought a request up during Bible study or over lunch, I'd say the obligatory, "I'll pray for you." And sometimes I would, but most of the time I completely forgot about their request and cared little because how much would my prayer do anyway?

One morning while driving to Bible study, I tuned the radio to my favorite station. Just then, Lysa TerKeurst came on with a little sixty-second word of encouragement. I often listened and enjoyed her understanding of the Word as she saw God moving and alive in real-life situations. But this morning I turned it up as she spoke about "praying specifics." It opened my heart to specific prayer being completely acceptable in the eyes of the Lord.

I always thought I was being a good little Christian when immediately following a prayer request with, ". . . But Your will be done." That day, though, as I turned the knob of the radio louder, I was challenged to lift up specifics and be bold about the things I was praying fervently for. Yes, I want God's will to be done. And I always tell Him that His abundant knowledge of what's going on behind the scenes should outweigh my desires because He knows what is right and perfect.

Yet, sitting in the car listening to Lysa was the first moment I realized it was alright to be raw and real and strip away all the Christian niceties I had learned while growing up. Prayer was no longer stereotyped and sterilized, but suddenly felt solid and substantial.

I realized it was not only okay to ask the Lord for my deep desires, but He welcomed it.

Remembering to posture myself with a heart that said, *If I ever request something but You have something planned that is "more" and "bigger" than what I'm asking, interrupt and disregard my request,* I bowed before Him in a similar fashion to Hannah's passionate payer in 1 Samuel. Knowing our heavenly Father heard when she prayed that He would open her womb and give her a son, I began to bring my hidden hunger into the light and told Him of my desire of being with Imani at the end of October for my birthday. I even began to add the crazy idea of bringing her home before Christmas into my conversation and time of communion with Him.

Before I had prayed specifics over our children and over situations in our family's life and in the lives of others, and He answered and poured out blessing. As time went on, though, I became ashamed that I prayed specifics when I was in crisis but subpar in the normal day-to-day. I didn't come to the Lord as often as I felt I should, yet I continued to feel God tell me to be more of a woman of prayer. But for the most part, I felt like I failed at it miserably.

WHY? Why is it so hard just to pray? I'd often ask myself. *Praying isn't difficult, it's simply talking. And we all know I like to talk . . . so just talk to God. What's the big deal? I think I'm lazy. Maybe that's it?*

Frustrated, I began using the concept of praying specifically for the *desire* to pray more. To give me an urgency about it. And He has.

Through the honest request of *wanting* to pray more, He has given me a passion for it. I have far to go and would love to one day be considered a "prayer warrior," but there is no denying He is answering my specific request as my relationship with Him deepens.

For the past several years, the Lord has begun to impress people onto my heart. Out of the blue I'll suddenly have someone's name roll through my consciousness. Sometimes it's someone I know, but more often than not I don't even recognize who it is. And stranger still, it's typically a first and last name. A very specific person.

I feel an unexplainable urgency to pray for the person who belongs to that name. It's not something I can put off. When I have these names pressed deeply upon my heart, it feels critical they're covered in prayer at that exact moment.

Sometimes it's an individual who appears to have immediate needs that I can pray for. Like a man I saw a few weeks ago sleeping on the cold sidewalk beneath the overpass where I drove while running errands. Something serious is going on in this young man's life that needs prayer. Perhaps it's a prayer for something as simple as food or shelter or a warm coat. Or maybe it's something deeper like healed relationships or to know that he's loved and of great value.

Other times it's the man in the car next to me at the stoplight. Or the woman by my side on the treadmill. Or that individual whose cart just passed me at the grocery store. We can't often see people's hurts and struggles and fears. We're so good at hiding them, aren't we?

And yet God specifically handpicks people He wants us to pray for. Their wounds and joys and circumstances are known to our Father, and we need to do our best to remain in tune with Him so when He prompts even a quick little prayer for someone, we are aligned with Him and can feel that prompting.

> When we spend time in His Word and in prayer, we show our desire to live in alignment with Him.

I'm not saying I always get it. I'm sure there are hundreds of times every day when I'm so caught up in my own thoughts and busyness that I miss someone He would really like me to lift up in prayer. But I try. I often have the radio off when I'm alone, and I try to listen in the silence of the day: in the shower, the car, during the walk from the elliptical to the child-care area. You, too, can use those silences to listen to Christ's promptings.

A few nights ago I had one of those dreams that lasts all night. I even woke up several times and went right back into the dream, which for me never happens.

I was seeing a woman kidnapped and sold into the sex trade. I experienced, as an unnoticed bystander, the horror that was now her life. And even in my dream I felt God ask me to pray. I had a horrible time dragging myself out of bed that morning as I felt a deep connection to this young woman and two others who had joined her horrible circumstance. Over and over in my mind and in my heart—even without yet being completely conscious and awake—I prayed the simple words, *Get them out. Lord . . . GET THEM OUT.* All morning, all day really, I prayed that simple prayer with intense fervor.

I don't know if I was seeing someone's actual story unfold. Perhaps it was simply God urging me to pray over this horrific form of slavery as a whole. But what I do know is that our Father asked me to pray.

And *that* I can do.

> *You can pray while you work. Work doesn't stop prayer*
> *and prayer doesn't stop work. It requires only*
> *that small raising of the mind to him: I love you God,*
> *I trust you, I believe in you, I need you now.*
> *Small things like that. They are wonderful prayers.*
> Mother Teresa

And I think that's how God likes it, because by praying in this way, we're asking Him to be part of our every day. The mundane portions, as well as the tear-filled ones. When we spend time in His Word and in prayer, we show our desire to live in alignment with Him. He knows He can call on us to intercede on behalf of someone and we'll obey even in the chaos and busyness of the day.

It may seem like such a simple or insignificant thing. But I assure you, it is the furthest thing from little. He does great, monumental things when people pray. He heals hearts, minds, bodies, relationships, and breaks chains of inadequacy, fear, and addiction.

Believe it.

Cling to it.

> *"The world is full of so-called prayer warriors*
> *who are prayer-ignorant. They're full of formulas*
> *and programs and advice, peddling techniques for getting*
> *what you want from God. Don't fall for that nonsense.*

This is your Father you are dealing with,
and he knows better than you what you need.
With a God like this loving you, you can pray very simply."
Matthew 6:7–8 MSG

When I do stop, even if it's just for a moment during a chaos-filled day, I know that I'm engaging with God and something amazing happens: I enter into the presence of God. Sometimes nothing even needs to be said; I just need to be still. In those moments I think of the long-loved hymn written from Psalm 46: "Be still, and know that I am God" (v. 10 ESV).

In the silence of the heart God speaks.
If you face God in prayer and silence, God will speak to you.
Then you will know that you are nothing.
It is only when you realize your nothingness, your emptiness,
that God can fill you with Himself.
Souls of prayer are souls of great silence.
Mother Teresa

At first glance, we may think that being still is contradictory to an engrained American culture of busy, busier, busiest. But just because one thing seems opposite doesn't mean it is. It's not either/or. We can be dancing while still being still. Whether we're physically still while calming our hearts or not, we can allow the world to just fall away as we worship our Lord. In Mother Teresa's quote above, and others throughout this chapter, she talks about the silence of the heart, and that's exactly what's needed. Though admittedly it is easier for me to hear Him best in quiet surroundings, we need to simply enjoy being in the presence of the King of the universe. It is with a still heart that we will hear His still, small voice (1 Kings 19:12).

Like Ann Voskamp said in her book *One Thousand Gifts,*

The world I live in is loud and blurring and the toilets plug and I get speeding tickets and the dog gets sick all over the back step and I forget everything and these six kids lean hard into me all day to teach and raise and lead and I fail hard and there are real souls that are at stake and how long do I really have to figure out how to live full of grace, full of joy—before these six beautiful children fly the coop and my mothering days fold up quiet. How do you open the eyes to see how to take the daily, domestic, workday vortex and invert it into the dome of an everyday cathedral? Could I go back to my life and pray with eyes wide open?[11]

In 1 Thessalonians 5:17, Paul encouraged us to . . .

Pray continually. (NIV)
Pray constantly. (VOICE)
Pray without ceasing. (ESV)

Whichever way you slice it, Paul was asking us to pray. All. The. Time. All throughout the day means during our quiet time with Him with and in worshipful movement. It can be specific and fervent, and it can be in such grief that words are not spoken at all. Whether verbally spoken or allowing the Holy Spirit to intercede for us (Romans 8:26–27), we have access to the throne of God at all times. And when we lift thanks, requests, and adoration up to Him, He is actively listening to every word.

. . . .

CHAPTER 10

Outside My Comfort Zone

. . . . . . 🦢 . . . .

God is looking for people to use,
and if you can get usable,
he will wear you out.
The most dangerous prayer you can pray is this:
"Use me."

RICK WARREN

Ben and I both want to live lives that don't center around ourselves or our comfort. We prayed years ago (and still pray today) for God to use us to make a difference in the lives of others, that we would constantly have our door open. When the words, *Use me* and *Send me* first escaped our lips, we had no idea what it would look like when He did.

Our Lord has asked Ben and me to do so many things out of our comfort zones, outside our humanly planned first-choice desires. So much so, in fact, that at this point when things seem smooth and we're settling into a rose-colored season, I feel I'm not hearing the Lord correctly and jump deeper into the Word and my time of prayer with Him.

I want to make sure I'm not drifting in a life I built myself. Perhaps at some point God will grant me the gift of rest outside of Sabbath and I won't feel this so intensely, but I have a feeling it won't be on this side of heaven. Why should it be? Every day He reminds me, *I didn't put you in this world to be content. I put you in this world to make a difference for My kingdom.*

One morning while having some time of quiet with my Lord, I felt a prompting to dig into what contentment truly meant and what He wanted it to signify for me.

> *I am not saying this because I am in need, for I have learned to be content whatever the circumstance.*
> Philippians 4:11 NIV

When searching my thesaurus for the word *content*, I saw what I expected—it means to be fulfilled, willing, and satisfied.[12] I love that it says "willing," don't you? Yes, Lord, I *am willing*. I will be content in what You will. I will be satisfied.

Continuing to other synonyms, however, my eyes stopped on the words *comfortable, complacent, smug,* and the phrase *fat and happy.*

Wow.

Pretty sure that's not *at all* what we're supposed to be.

I think it's so easy for us to be content with how our lives are playing out. Sure, we want this . . . and that change would be nice, but all in all, life is fine. We don't want to rock the boat. We're content.

Admittedly, when I'm soul weary there are times I actually crave the fat and happy idea. Sometimes I'm tired and the concept of being complacent doesn't sound too bad. But I don't think that's the contentment God desires of us.

In my heart, I know it's when He stretches me and I have no choice but to lean heavily on Him that I need to be content. Content with knowing *His* plan is the *best* plan. Unconditional contentment even in the wait. Even in the midst of pain. Even while taking up residence in the valley. It's thriving like we learned about in Jeremiah 29.

If our flames grow dim, it means there's so much life we're missing. In 2 Timothy 1:6 (ESV), Paul reminded us "to fan into flame the gift of God, which is in you . . ." By using this particular visual, Paul made it abundantly clear to his friend Timothy (and now to us) that if we do not tend to the fire, fanning it to keep it ablaze, it will go out. Not that God will cease to love us or invite us in, but that *our* love for *Him* can flicker out. That's not what I want . . . and I have a feeling that's not what you want either.

I traveled to Dallas recently to spend time with Christian women from around the country at an annual conference called IF:Lead. My friend, Tatum, wanted me to connect with her sister while there since she was also attending. I quickly learned she had only been a Christian for about a year. There was something distinct about this girl and it took only moments to realize what it was: she was ablaze. Her spirit was incandescent, and I was drawn to her like a moth to a flame. I wanted what she had. The funny thing is that she felt the same about me. Sitting together waiting for a workshop to begin, she shared how little she feels like she knows about God and the Bible but she wanted to know it all. I imagined her sitting on the bank of a great pool of water with a straw in her mouth, drawing Christ's knowledge and wisdom deep into her very being. She was a sponge and she knew it, wanting Him and nothing less than everything He had to give.

When she said she wanted what I had, it was for a different reason than mine. She perceived that I had the knowledge already, that because I'd known Him longer, I knew more. And though I may have more comprehension of the Scriptures, I told her that she knew more than she realized. She was a glowing example of His love and His grace. Tatum told me later that she's a different person with Christ steering her life and it's as if the real, more complete her has now stepped out.

That is what I want. And it was exactly what Paul was hinting at. The spirit within this girl was dazzling and resplendent, and so should ours be. Yet how do we move past the mountaintop experience of being a new Christian, or having just come home from a Christian retreat or camp, and keep that flame gleaming bright?

We keep getting to know Him.

You "know" your parents, your friends, your boyfriend, or your husband, but you also have the desire to continue learning and growing and knowing more about them because you love them. It should be the same with God. We can't say we "know" Him and stop there. That's not a true relationship; that's merely interest that breeds indifference.

We must fan the flame in our relationship with the Lord by spending time with Him in prayer and learning who He really is, as well as living a life that reflects our trust and faith in Him. Even if responding to His request means nothing will ever be the same, we must stir the embers and say yes.

During the months of waiting before bringing Imani home, a quiet tapping eventually exploded into a deep ache, knowing this was only the beginning of the expansion of our family. The realization that Christ was asking us to release the windowsill and make another scary-feeling jump forced us to live even further outside our comfort zones. The thought of it made me tremble.

Just when I thought I'd made so much progress in hearing God's voice and obeying His promptings, the bigness of what He was requiring of Ben and me made me take a few steps back. Back into the fears of my youth.

Can I be really raw and vulnerable with you for a minute? Because I think there's (at least) one thing in our lives we pray against. Something we don't want to do or be part of. A place where we don't want to get our hands dirty. Maybe it's too big. Or too seemingly painful. Perhaps the scariness is simply the unknown of it. Or perhaps we pray against it because we know that with the acceptance of this calling, life will become the opposite of what we've worked so hard to create.

For me, this thing was Africa.

Christians rarely admit that they pray against going to serve Christ in a particular place, but I did. I did not want to be called to Africa. I was scared of the poverty, the extreme without. I was afraid of the disease and the children whose faces are covered with flies and who have sickened feet without the protection of shoes. It was a scary, unknown continent where missionaries wear long skirts and wraps in their hair. There's dust. Lots of dust. And maybe disease-bearing mosquitos. And Ebola.

Yes, there are those beautiful smiles from those beautiful dark faces. Those eyes that show both pain and joy. But still, I secretly prayed, *Jesus, anywhere. Anywhere . . . but Africa.*

And so I went about my days and perhaps prayed for the people of Sudan or Uganda when I thought of it, but as I prayed, deep down I was scared that if I spent too much time praying, God would somehow think maybe He should send me there. So I made my prayers quick.

Even having lived in Guatemala and seeing poverty firsthand, I pushed memories from my mind, forcing myself to become numb. Since that part of my life wasn't embraced by most around me, I compartmentalized those experiences, almost pretending they didn't happen.

I'm horrified to tell you that in my heart I'd roll my eyes when members of yet another mission trip returned telling of the "wonderful" and "amazing" things they saw in Kenya, Sierra Leone, and Ghana. How God was moving there and they were honored to be part of it. Genuinely, from the bottom of my heart, I prayed I would not have to have anything to do with Africa.

I didn't recognize it then, but everything changed the day I sat on that wooden park bench overlooking Seattle's Space Needle. The day I laid my plans at Jesus's feet and told Him to take the pen I was writing my own life with and altered the direction of my future.

Not my will, but Yours, Father. Use me—really, really use me. I was as serious about it at that moment as I am today.

I'm not going to tell you that I suddenly loved children and woke up one day wanting a big family. Nor did I immediately feel a tug toward Africa. I didn't even know I was yet to give up on my dream to be an art curator.

But little by little, Christ revealed Himself to me.

Just like Christ has adopted each of us into His family, as Ben and I grew in our faith, we realized we wanted to adopt and pour love into these kids who may not otherwise have any. And He just kept opening up my selfish heart. And opening and opening and opening. He's still opening it, urging it wider with His good and graciously patient hands.

There have been so many "I'd never" moments that have turned into "I cannot wait" ones. Disgust into desire. Unlove into deep, deep passion.

And it's not because I prayed I wouldn't be sent to Africa. Though I envision Him sitting up in heaven, chuckling and rolling His eyes at me for the thousandth time, I don't think my passion came from my fear and disregard of this continent full of history and beautiful people. It came because He knew I was made to be a mom to my kids, for He knew their future already. He knew the sweet mamas of other little loves who would one day need us to care for their children.

Christ knew we would be a listening ear to countless families going through international adoptions and that we were to raise awareness to it, particularly toward adopting older children. Our life and our callings and passions aren't because God is trying to give us our greatest fears. He doesn't feel powerful granting us our dread.

What He *does* do, though, when we genuinely want nothing more than the life He's designed for us, is change our very hearts. He knows our giftings and where we could be used best.

> *For you created my inmost being;*
> *you knit me together in my mother's womb.*
> Psalm 139:13 NIV

He's the One who created us! Wouldn't He be the perfect One to tell us how our gifts and loves and passions could best be utilized? Even those passions we haven't quite uncovered or discovered yet will be used. If we let Him, the Lord will give our hearts a new song, a new purpose, and deep, deep desires.

Sometimes it is similar to something we're already doing, combining with things we already love. But other times—as in my case—He simply throws out all the old to make room for the new.

And the new is so much more fulfilling and true than anything I could have planned on my own.

So Africa? I'm no longer scared of you. My prayers have changed from pleading not to set foot on your soil to begging that He gives me another opportunity to run in your direction. Your people are joyful and generous, your history rich and deep. And your land is so much more beautiful than I could've imagined. I want your scent to rub off on me. I want more of you.

> *You will again obey the LORD and follow*
> *all his commands I am giving you today.*
> *Then the LORD your God will make you*
> *most prosperous in all the work*
> *of your hands and in the fruit of your womb,*
> *the young of your livestock and the crops of your land.*
> *The LORD will again delight in you and make you prosperous,*
> *just as he delighted in your ancestors,*
> *if you obey the LORD your God and keep his commands*
> *and decrees that are written in this Book of the Law*
> *and turn to the LORD your God with*
> *all your heart and with all your soul.*
> Deuteronomy 30:8–10 NIV

I was talking to a friend earlier today who has a nonprofit in Uganda. We were chatting about how strange it is to be homesick and long for a place that has never been our home. "It's my heart's home," she said. *Yes*, I thought. *YES*. She gets it. She, too, has had her heart fixed and changed and transformed according to the life Christ put her on this earth for.

Yes.

Jesus, forever yes.

Change our hearts. Because with You, nothing is scary. Not even Africa.

Isn't it amazing that the comfort zones God asks each of us to live outside of are so varied? He calls us to such different things, gifting us with tremendously diverse passions.

A dear friend of mine works in television. Even when we were growing up, you could tell she was made for it. Though we'd met in preschool, she was one of the genuine girls I found after coming back home from Guatemala, wanting so desperately to fit in like I once had, yet struggling with the knowledge that I might not actually want to in the same way I did before.

Through the years, I've seen Megan covering Thursday Night Football and on television shows and movies. To me, she is my friend Meggie, but to those who see her on *Inside Edition*, she is known as Megan Alexander, the woman who meets and interviews incredible world changers, dresses for the red carpet, and travels the world. From the outside looking in, her life of fame looks exciting, yet what we don't see is all the behind-the-scenes occurrences where she holds on to the Lord with white knuckles. He uses her in great ways, but as He does, He's strengthening her trust in Him while calling her out of her comfort zone nearly every day. Inviting her into the folds of His calling through day-to-day hard work and sweat, God gifts her with an extreme passion for her job and the ministry it's provided for her and her family. God has given her a seat at a table most of us aren't invited to, but Megan uses the opportunities He's given her to shine bright for Him in all she does.

The different life paths Megan and I are on remind me of the passage in 1 Corinthians that speaks of one body with many parts.

Just as a body, though one, has many parts, but all its many parts form one body, so it is with Christ. . . . Even so the body is not made up of one part but of many. Now if the foot should say, "Because I am not a hand, I do not belong to the body," it would not for that reason stop being part of the body. And if the ear should say, "Because I am not an eye, I do not belong to the body," it would not for that reason stop being part of the body. If the whole body were an eye, where would the sense of hearing be? If the whole body were an ear, where would the sense of smell be? But in fact God has placed the parts in the body, every one of them, just as he wanted them to be.

1 Corinthians 12:12, 14–18 NIV

Society often puts adoptive moms on a pedestal we don't deserve. Similarly, we may think my sweet friend Megan is a more impressive and important part of the body because she's on TV and meets with impactful and famous people every day.

We may feel unimportant as we settle into our cubicle each morning at a job we're not thrilled with.

Maybe we'll find ourselves at the grocery store for the second time that day, and we will also most certainly reach into the closet for the broom and dustpan because, for the twelfth time today, snacks have been spilled by grubby little hands still figuring out how to eat by themselves, and at the end of the day we find ourselves scrolling through social media fawning over the moms who appear to have it all together.

Rather than comparing ourselves to others, let's instead be challenged and encouraged by the words of Paul in that passage above.

We are every bit as important to the body of Christ as Megan, Mother Teresa, Billy Graham, our pastors, missionaries, or so many others we look up to.

We each have different callings—and that's good.

It's biblical.

It's important.

Who wants a body full of hands anyway? Weird.

Living a life outside our comfort zone is more about how our heart is positioned than where we are physically placed.

There's something about this quote that makes my throat tighten up and my heart ache:

> *If a man is called to be a street sweeper, he should sweep streets*
> *even as Michelangelo painted, or Beethoven composed music*
> *or Shakespeare wrote poetry. He should sweep streets so well*
> *that all the hosts of heaven and earth will pause to say,*
> *"Here lived a great street sweeper who did his job well."*
> Martin Luther King Jr.[13]

Amen, Dr. King. *Amen.*

My grandfather worked for Wonder Bread and Mother's Cookies for most of his adult life (which, side note, was pretty much the coolest job a grandpa could have—he was always letting us jump up into his big delivery truck and choose whatever package of cookies we wanted). My grandpa, whom we all appropriately call "Cookie," is like this street sweeper Dr. King describes. Most people probably wouldn't care much about a job as a cookie distributor. But Grandpa Cookie did his job better than well. He did it with excellence. He did it with great pride.

> Don't allow anyone to make you second-guess what you're positive Christ has put on your heart.

Instead of simply going about his job, Cookie went outside his comfort zone and learned details about the individuals he came in contact with throughout his days. He knew everyone who worked in each and every store and he knew their stories. He *knew* them and joked with them and fellowshiped with them.

He shared life with them.

It wasn't about the cookies he lined up so neatly on the grocery store shelves. It was about the people.

He has made a difference in the lives of so many. He has long since retired, but even still, years later, when I would visit Seattle and swing by our neighborhood QFC grocery store, I was greeted with questions of how Cookie was doing. Stories would then be retold, which always seem to end in laughter when Cookie was involved. Because Grandpa Cookie tells jokes and people love him.

Cookie is someone who lives out the example Jesus set when He walked the earth. Warmhearted and caring.

Cookie and Megan and you and me, we're different. I was called to adoption and to have a houseful of children and to write a book and blog.

You are likely called to do something completely different. Something God has planned and *equally* as important.

Please, please don't allow anyone to belittle your calling.

Don't allow anyone to make you second-guess what you're positive Christ has put on your heart. Whether it's something huge and daunting, something that's a bit scary and seems bigger than you can actually accomplish, or something that others may think *isn't big enough.*

> *"My thoughts are nothing like your thoughts," says the* LORD.
> *"And my ways are far beyond anything you could imagine.*
> *For just as the heavens are higher than the earth,*
> *so my ways are higher than your ways*
> *and my thoughts higher than your thoughts."*
> Isaiah 55:8–9 NLT

Whether the Lord has called you to be the crossing guard at your kid's school, work with recovering addicts in the inner city, begin a Bible study for college girls, or start a jewelry business partnering with artisan entrepreneurs to make a difference in some of the world's most vulnerable communities—it's all important.

Why?

Because the Lord has asked you to do it.

And that's enough.

PART FOUR

Openhanded Trust

CHAPTER 11

It's Your Calling, Not Theirs

.......🦢.......

Obviously, I'm not trying to win the approval of people,
but of God. If pleasing people were my goal,
I would not be Christ's servant.
Dear brothers and sisters,
I want you to understand that the gospel message
I preach is not based on mere human reasoning.
I received my message from no human source,
and no one taught me. Instead,
I received it by direct revelation from Jesus Christ.

GALATIANS 1:10–12 NLT

For years I've heard people say, "God will never give you something you cannot handle." And for a long time I actually thought it was in the Bible (it's not, by the way). The more I think about it, the more I disagree with this frequently given response to someone's struggles. Why on earth would God give us things we can accomplish on our own? If that were true, we wouldn't need Him, and one of God's chief desires for us is a deep hunger, knowing there is no way we can make it without His help.

While aligning myself with what God wants for my life, rather than what I *think* I want, or even what other people think I should do or want, I have realized if I sense a prompting that seems a bit crazy—it's probably from God! He's not typically going to call us to do something easy or mundane, but rather something that will stretch us and force us to lean on Him.

When Ben and I were in the paperwork stage of the adoption process, long before Imani was a reality, we began praying about the age of the child or children we were to adopt. We realized God was turning our hearts toward not only a baby girl but also an older boy, between five and seven years old.

We frequented the "Waiting Child List," which could be accessed through our agency's website. After putting little Anton and Laith down to bed at night, Ben and I would snuggle on the couch with our laptop and scroll through the photos of the sweet faces of the precious older children who were paper-ready and waiting for a family to choose them. We'd pray over each child as we searched their faces and read their medical history, hoping for any other little nugget of information about each child the agency listed.

One of those evenings we happened upon a little boy named Temesgen. There was just something about him. We couldn't describe why, but we needed to know more. During this time, we fell on our knees, spending the next several weeks engulfed in prayer, seeking wisdom from friends and family members, and we asked for their prayers of discernment as well.

We were shocked when every single person we asked wisdom from told us not to go forward in adopting an older child. Apparently going outside the birth order is a *huge* no-no and would be "psychologically destructive to our current children." They would be displaced and forever negatively impacted. We had constant conversations that held serious undertones of "Your naïveté will ruin you" and sat knee to knee with the people closest and dearest to us as they literally said, "You will destroy your family."

Our family and friends, who are largely very godly people, with amazing personal relationships with our Lord and Savior, were all very concerned and strongly against what we were thinking about doing, even though we said we thought it was a prompting from God.

We weren't naïve; we understood this wouldn't be all sunshine and rainbows. The magnitude of this idea wasn't lost on us, but as the amount of negative unanimous advisement we received increased, our confidence in what the Lord had impressed upon our hearts wavered. In its place, discouraged and befuddled thoughts took hold and gripped tightly.

The short of it is, we got scared. We greatly considered their opinions and certainly didn't want to destroy our family. Surely God wouldn't ask us to do something so crazy, we told ourselves. We figured we were coming into this conviction of adoption with a "go big or go home" mentality, which was fine when purchasing a Thanksgiving turkey, yet horrible when family planning. Perhaps we were just those stereotypical Americans who wanted to swoop in and save the day.

During that time of prayer and wisdom seeking, a DVD complete with photos and short videos of little Temesgen arrived on our door-step. We decided we didn't want to watch it, knowing we would fall in love with the little boy and we had already decided he wasn't the right fit for our family. After eyeing the envelope on the kitchen counter for several days, I finally wavered and ripped it open and watched it one afternoon with Anton and Laith.

It was a very short film featuring the cutest little Ethiopian boy with a shaved head saying his ABCs in strongly accented English and playing soccer within the walls of the orphanage. Anton and Laith instantly wanted him to be their brother. My heart ached as I watched it. *Oh Lord, this is surely* not *our son, right? We've prayed and prayed and sought wisdom and advice from so many people, including folks who have opened their homes to older children. They're all telling us how hard it is, how this will negatively affect Anton and Laith, displacing them and messing up the birth order of our family. But, Lord, is he . . . is he our son?*

I sent the DVD back that next week with a little note saying, "Thank you so much for sharing this video. Sadly, I don't think he's the right fit for our family." And with that note, we closed the door. That was that. It made sense. It was practical. This little boy would find another home. *You'll take care of him, I know You will. Right, God? Just not in our family.*

Days and weeks ticked by. Months passed, and as they did, we pushed our decision with Temesgen from our minds. Then, suddenly, we got "the call" about Imani, and as we prepared ourselves for the trip to get Imani and bring her home from Ethiopia, a call from the director of our agency brought word of Temesgen. We were surprised when she brought him up since it had been four months since I'd sent back that video. "Temesgen has been moved from an orphanage many hours away, to one in the capital about fifteen minutes away from the guesthouse where you'll be staying. Do you want to meet him? He'd have no idea you'd be there to see him. Bring jump ropes and candy with you," she urged. "The kids will simply think you're there to play with them and are taking a tour of the orphanage."

Ben and I hadn't talked about Temesgen since we had decided not to go forward with an older child. Not once. And as I found out later, I somehow neglected to tell Ben that the boys and I had even watched the video. As we prayed and shared together now, Ben divulged that he had thought about and prayed for Temesgen nearly every day during the months after we had closed the door on bringing him into our family. I looked at my husband incredulously, sharing that I also thought about and prayed for him nearly daily.

Looking back, it's shocking that we never talked about Temesgen during all those months, when he was so obviously on our hearts. God was apparently preparing us individually because it was quickly evident that we needed to carefully reopen the door and prayerfully examine our true intent in bringing this not-so-little boy into our family. We decided that we'd pack small toys, bubbles, gum, and such, and spend a few hours with the kids at Temesgen's orphanage and to see if we heard anything from God.

And boy, did we.

After traveling nearly two days, Ben and I filed out of the last of many airplanes it had taken to get to Ethiopia. Standing restlessly and hungrily, irritated by the slow immigration line, and then wading through the men who promised to find and carry our bags for a few *birr* (Ethiopian currency), we finally found the driver from our guesthouse. As we settled wearily yet excitedly into the squeaky seats, our driver turned around, asking where we'd like to go first. Smiling at one another, we decided to ignore our rumbling stomachs and tired eyes. Gulping down the protein bars and dried mango we'd brought for the flights, we rode off to see Temesgen. Little did we know, this moment would be one of many pendulums that would swing us away from any sort of ordinary, comfortable life.

Heading straight for Resurrection, the perfectly named orphanage, would change our lives forever. Rebirth and restoration were at our fingertips.

As we drove in through the rusted, squeaky metal gate and onto the grounds of the orphanage, little Temesgen was the first child to run out from the white stone block building, jumping the entire bank of stairs as he rushed to greet us. Dressed in a dirty, white sleeveless T-shirt, ill-fitting cargo shorts, and (much) too small girl's flip-flops, he immediately began to kick a well-loved soccer ball around with Ben. As I stood by the van, watching the two of them play and laugh together, I heard the voice of God whisper in my ear.

This is your son.

Whaaaattt? No. No, Lord. I don't think so.

This is your son, He whispered in my ear again.

I just stood there having an internal wrestling match with God as I tried to convince Him that He had no idea what He was saying. Why it made no sense.

This is your son, was His only reply. He said it over and over as I continued to watch the kids play with Ben, joy emanating from each of their faces.

. . . and it finally sunk in.

It was like reading that first pregnancy test all over again. But instead of freaking out and saying, "I'm PREGNANT!" I was instead crying out, "He's my SON!" The very moment I actually accepted the word the Lord gave me, love and joy washed over me and took my fears away.

Gone was the consternation, the anxiety and confusion surrounding bringing home an older child. As I stood watching him and Ben play, little and big girls swarmed with the desire to touch my blonde hair and to braid it as beautifully as their own. At that moment, it seemed almost laughable that my fear had dictated how I obeyed God. This was a wild and brazen life He was asking of us, I concluded, one contrary to anything typical and conventional.

Deciding to listen to God rather than the well-intentioned men and women in our lives, I hurried away from the opinion of anyone else. If this was the path God asked us to walk, I would most certainly take His hand and step into it.

I prayed Ben felt the same.

You'd think I'd have gushed all about my conversation with the Lord the moment Ben and I loaded back into the van. Strangely, the moment was so monumental, I couldn't bring myself to say it aloud. I wasn't any less elated by the revelation, and doubt wasn't even making the tiniest debut; the epiphany was simply still being etched upon my heart. It was something so precious that I couldn't bring myself to divulge it in spoken voice.

We sped on to another area of town, where Imani's orphanage was located. It took all my emotional strength to keep from sobbing as her nanny placed her back into my arms. It had been weeks, but it felt like centuries since I'd snuggled her. My jagged heart suddenly felt plump and whole, like it could beat again. But I was sad and upset that she was still so ill, even though we had left plenty of medicine and formula for her when we said good-bye after our Ethiopian court trip. Looking into the dark ochre of her eyes, I vowed we would do everything within our power to help her get well, praying God would use His power.

When we weren't pestering the US Embassy in hopes that they would expedite her visa and passport because she was extremely ill, most of our week was spent in and out of the hospital and at doctors' appointments. Imani's weakened body grieved us. Though five months old, she weighed a mere nine pounds. *Even preemie diapers are big on you*, I remember thinking while fastening them around her small waist, concerned how her skin literally hung from her bones. Standing firm through the profound sorrow in how her frame revealed the telltale bloated stomach of a malnourished child, I prayed for her health with every breath.

Because we were consumed in finding help for her infected lungs and emaciated body, conversation of Temesgen simply didn't happen until the night before our flight home.

"What do you think?" Ben asked me as Imani slept on his chest and we reclined in bed. Still not quite ready to admit the hugeness of this new calling upon our family, I responded, "Well, I know one hundred percent what I think, but I want to hear it out of your mouth first."

Ben shared exactly what I had felt the Lord impress upon my heart. After praying together and taking a deep breath, we jumped again. Calling our in-country lawyer, we began the process of bringing Temesgen home. The next morning before our flight we drove back over to Resurrection to spend the day with him before flying home with Imani. We have the most precious photo of the woman in charge of the orphanage telling our son that these crazy white people he played with a few days prior were actually his parents. The look on his face is pure delight with widened eyes and open mouthed smile. Leaving him that afternoon and placing his life once again into our Father's hands was as hard as it was good. Temesgen's new daddy and I may have been flying home, but we rested in the fact that his heavenly Father cared about him even more than we did.

While still in Ethiopia and for months after coming home, Temesgen mentioned wanting to change his name. It's not unusual for older kids to want to do this because it's their own way to embrace their new life. New life, new name. In the Bible when God redirected someone's path or gave them a larger purpose for their lives, their name would also be changed to signify this transformation in the direction of their lives. For example, Abram became Abraham when he was told he would father a nation, and Saul became Paul when he turned from persecuting and killing Christians to committing his entire life to Jesus instead (Genesis 17:4–5; Acts 9, 13:9).

We didn't want to change Temesgen's name though, and we had no intention of doing so. It was all he had of his past and of his heritage. It was different than changing Ada'a to Imani, because someone at the orphanage named her. There was no real meaning or significance. Temesgen, though, means "the sighing within your soul in thankfulness to God." His mama named him that; she wanted him to grow up knowing he was loved so much that the deepest recesses of her soul thanked the Lord for him. There was significance in that name I wasn't willing to give up.

And yet he just kept asking. It was obviously very important to him.

One hot San Antonio afternoon, our three little boys were skateboarding on the sidewalk in front of our house. Bringing a picnic blanket and mixing bowl of cool water for Imani to splash in, I also grabbed a now-dusty baby name book from the bookshelf along with a notebook and pen, and headed outside to join them. Temesgen had been particularly persistent in asking for a new name the past several days, and even more so that morning. Starting in the As, I'd call out names to him that I liked, and others I thought he'd view as funny because of his profound accent. ". . . Colby? . . . David? . . . Fernando?" I leafed back and forth through the pages, and I came to a Biblical name section and called out "How about Ezekiel?" Hearing the name, he hopped off his skateboard, paused, and looked at me. "Yes. Ezekiel," he said. I wrote the name below the others he'd shown interest in, ready to move on to the next page in the book. Instead though, my little boy came over to me, pointed to the name I had just written, and gently closed the book in my lap. "Ezekiel," he said again.

And that was that. Ezekiel Temesgen Sampson Anderson. His dad's name was Sampson; his birth name, of course, is Temesgen. His new names bookend the heart and significance of his past. Ezekiel, by the way, means "God strengthens." It's so appropriate in connection with his dad's name, Samson, another Biblical figure known for his great strength (Judges 13–16). God was showing early on what a incredible force our son would be.

Remember the lesson the Lord taught me through my lack of desire to learn the basics of piano? I felt like this assignment from God to bring an older child into our family was God acknowledging that Ben and I had worked on our foundation. And we were ready for Him to put us in charge of something larger (see Matthew 25:21). With the notion that our heavenly Father never intended those committed to Him to feel comfortable and safe, we were all in.

Ben and I often remind each other that this isn't an easy road the Lord has asked us to walk, but it's a road He asked us loud and clear to take. And because of that, following Him is the least complicated thing I've ever done.

I said least complicated. Not easy.

When we got home and began to share our news, everyone around us thought we were doing too much, too fast. The word *naïve* was again thrown around as friends and family warned us of the consequences in having two toddlers, bringing home a baby girl from Ethiopia, and then deciding right away to also adopt a six-year-old.

They continued to tell us, "You're going to destroy your family." But we knew with overwhelming confidence that this was what God was calling us to do, so we just smiled, said, "Thanks for the advice," and continued on with His plan, praying and gripping Christ and His faithfulness with white knuckles, all the way.

So what do you do when no one supports you in what you know, without a doubt, is what the Lord has required of you?

You trust.

Trust God from the bottom of your heart; don't try to figure out everything on your own. Listen for God's voice in everything you do, everywhere you go; he's the one who will keep you on track.
Proverbs 3:5–6 MSG

It sounds a little cliché, though, doesn't it? It sounds so simple, so streamlined and easy, wrapped up in a pretty little box with white satin ribbon holding it tightly together.

Trust.

Trust even when things are scary, even when you have no idea how it's going to work out, even when your friends and family don't necessarily support your calling.

For we are God's masterpiece. He has created us anew in Christ Jesus, so we can do the good things he planned for us long ago.
Ephesians 2:10 NLT

I love going back to The Message version of the Bible when I want to read a passage in a new light.

Now God has us where he wants us, with all the time in this world and the next to shower grace and kindness upon us in Christ Jesus. Saving is all his idea, and all his work. All we do is trust him enough to let him do it. It's God's gift from start to finish! We don't play the major role. If we did, we'd probably go around bragging that we'd done the whole thing! No, we neither make nor save ourselves. God does both the making and saving. He creates each of us by Christ Jesus to join him in the work he does, the good work he has gotten ready for us to do, work we had better be doing.
Ephesians 2:7–10

He's got this! We just need to say yes and hold on tight.

Really, really tight.

Remember, this is your calling, not theirs. Who are you going to let run your life: well-meaning friends and family, or God?

As a parent myself, I see how often I desire ease and comfort for our children. We don't want our kids to go through struggles and hard things. We like the idea of lessening blows and strife. We want our little ones to be happy, right?

I think this was what our family and friends were doing. With loving hearts, they were attempting to steer us away from hard things. Ben and I have realized over time, though, that we need to prepare our children for the road, not the road for our children.

Who are we, then, to desire an easy life for ourselves, our families, and those around us? By urging the "safe" or the "easy," we are robbing others of the profound depth that can only come from clinging to Christ in affliction.

When Anton was six, I remember driving down a neighborhood road near our house. With him in his car seat behind me, we chatted back and forth about what it means to be brave. Our sweet son, who is now in the double digits, has always wanted to be in the military, specifically in the air force, and knows bravery is a prerequisite to what his heart yearns to do. As I asked how he'd describe bravery, he said simply, "It's being scared of something and doing it anyway."

When did my child get so smart?

First Corinthians 16:13 (NKJV) says, "Watch, stand fast in the faith, be brave, be strong." There are several elements to draw from in this short little verse.

1. *Watch:* Pay attention; be attentive. Be watchful of God's hand in things as He shows the path He's wanting you to take.
2. *Stand fast:* My thesaurus pairs this word with *withstand* and *resist.*[14] We need to recognize the need to weather the storm and grip tightly to our faith through it.
3. *Be brave:* Life is scary and sometimes really, really hard. There are some days when just getting out of bed makes my stomach

drop. It's okay if we're not fearless—be courageous through that fear instead.

4. *Be strong: Fortitude, vigor, toughness, vitality,* and *grit*—all these words are synonymous of *strength.*

Faith is the foundation of each of these. Faith breaks the chain of inadequacy and the fear that often surrounds.

Never think that you're too young or old, too uneducated, or somehow unworthy to make a difference. Years ago, when my sweet *farmor* (Swedish for "father's mother") was still alive, she shared her frustration with me as she felt "too old" to make much impact in the world. Entering into the eighth decade of her life for her felt futile as she spent more and more time at home while her health declined. I wish she knew then what we all know now: that God would use her until literally her last breath as she led her hospice nurse to the Lord a handful of days before God ushered her into His kingdom.

> Cling to Christ through insecurity and inadequacy, knowing He uses ordinary men and women (Acts 4:13).

There are things our children want to do and differences they want to make, and yet the world seems to say, "Not yet" and "You're too young." I've seen children's T-shirts floating around on social media with "Future World Changer" on them and I cringe. Why must we teach our children they have to be older and wiser in the dealings of our world before they can change it? Why can't they wear shirts that boast simply the words "World Changer" on them?

> *Don't let anyone belittle you because you are young.*
> *Instead, show the faithful, young and old,*
> *an example of how to live: set the standard for how*
> *to talk, act, love, and be faithful and pure.*
> 1 Timothy 4:12 VOICE

Though the community around us may decide we're ineffective or incapable in the areas God is leading us to, and may unintentionally even do their very best to cause us to think we're misinterpreting what He is asking of us, we must push away feelings of inadequacy that spring up in our minds. Push those *not enough* thoughts away and pray that the Lord will give you discernment. If you have peace even in the midst of a calling that seems rather crazy, you're likely living in obedience.

Knowing just where our insecurities lie, Satan will most certainly strike there first. Don't forget that our struggle isn't simply with obstacles that can be seen with our human eyes, but rather against evil in the heavenly realm (Ephesians 6:12), a realm that we don't usually have our eyes opened to, yet we live in the midst of.

Cling to Christ through insecurity and inadequacy, knowing He uses ordinary men and women (Acts 4:13). If He could prepare Moses to lead the Israelites out of Egypt, He can use all of us. We've already talked about how Moses tried to get out of what God asked him to do. With a head buzzing with insecurity and inadequacy, Satan whispered in his ear too.

But Moses said to God, "Who am I that I should go to Pharaoh
and bring the Israelites out of Egypt?"
Exodus 3:11 NIV

Moses answered, "What if they do not believe me or listen to me
and say, 'The LORD did not appear to you'?"
Exodus 4:1 NIV

Moses said to the LORD, "Pardon your servant, Lord.
I have never been eloquent, neither in the past nor since you have
spoken to your servant. I am slow of speech and tongue."
Exodus 4:10 NIV

But Moses said, "Pardon your servant, Lord.
Please send someone else."
Exodus 4:13 NIV

Over and over Moses questioned God's calling, even asking Him to send someone else! He, too, was afraid of his assignment from God. But let's believe God when He tells us to go somewhere, for He will have prepared a place for us, just as He had the Israelites. Exodus 23:20 tells of God sending an angel ahead of the Israelites to guard them along the way, guiding them to the place our heavenly Father had prepared. God commands that we get ourselves ready, pay close attention, and obey. God promises that if we do all these things, an angel strengthened by God Himself will fight for us. When you feel God calling you to do something that the world would think is crazy, get alone with God and pray:

Lord, help us keep our eyes open and tune our ears to You. Give us a hunger to obey You, and encourage a flaming desire to spend time in the Word that will be a constant, every day. Give us boldness and obedience. Don't allow us to keep our light under a bucket, to be hidden from the world. Because You, Father, will protect us. You will fight for us. Let us also fight for You.

Let us remember Your words in Romans 9:1, Father, and be encouraged by the possibility that You raised us up for this very purpose, that You may display Your power in us and that Your name may be proclaimed in all the earth.

Just when I'd become comfortable in what God had called us to—feeling as if I'd come so far—I realized that in reality, He was far from done. With the miraculous love and patience of Christ, my heart continued to be turned from stone and into flesh. He was not done stretching me; there was more I was to learn.

I want thy plan, O God, for my life.
May I be happy and contented whether
in the homeland or on the foreign field;
whether married or alone, in happiness or sorrow,
health or sickness, prosperity or adversity—I want Thy plan,
O God, for my life. I want it; oh I want it!
Oswald J. Smith[15]

CHAPTER 12

Fear Magnified

F.E.A.R. has two meanings:
Forget Everything and Run, or Face Everything and Rise.
The choice is yours.

UNKNOWN

When living our God-given calling or passion, we're not immune to the schemes of Satan. After all, the Bible tells us that he is the father of all lies, working diligently to steal our joy. I've learned through the years that if we're doing something that threatens the prince of darkness, you'd better believe we are walking around with a giant target on our backs.

I spoke at a Mothers of Preschoolers (MOPS) group recently and mentioned that I struggle with fear. As our morning together ended and ladies began filing out to pick up their children, one mom stopped me. Touching my arm tenderly, she said she couldn't believe fear was a stronghold for me.

She said, "It seems that you've done so many things outside most of our comfort zones that fear doesn't affect you. Before you admitted that, I figured God asks, and you simply obey. How can you say yes to Him so often and still live in the midst of fear?"

Saying yes to God's promptings, I explained, has nothing to do with having fear or not—it's how you respond in that fear. Time and time again, I must make the conscious decision to push fear aside, saying an internal, *No!* as if it's a mean bully trying to take me down. I've done some big, scary-feeling things through the years, and sometimes it's not even in those big decisions that the fear takes hold. Often it's during a normal day. The mundane Tuesday or random afternoon when I'm going about my business and I'm suddenly gripped with anxiety that feels like it's literally grabbing hold of my heart with talon fingers, squeezing tightly and cutting into me as my thoughts run wild about something that *might* happen.

I see Satan lurking in the darkness, watching. Waiting for the perfect time to strike. Because he's spent time observing how we go about our days, he knows where our weaknesses are and how to quickly snatch us.

Though I'd like to declare that we were full of smiles and high fives as we jumped up and said yes to adopting Ezekiel right away, the reality is different. Feeling deeply that Christ was asking us to bring home six-year-old Ezekiel mere months after Imani joined our family sent Ben and me spinning from the bigness of it all, especially because everyone we knew and loved disagreed with what we confidently believed we'd heard God say. Forgetting for a moment that we cannot stay where we are *and* go with God, our fear outweighed our obedience and we decided to stay safe. Shaking our heads in an emphatic *no way*, we refused the very God we had previously opened our hands to while pouring out the words, *Use me.*

Vulnerably pondering whether we believed God would grow us to be the people who could trust Him completely, we examined our hearts. What we found was a worship of contentment and a distaste for discomfort. Holding out our fears and weaknesses to Him to both expose them and ask Him to take them all, we rejoined our God in His adventure.

The first days of settling in with our new little six-year-old son were fun—an adventure, really. Everything was new and exciting with Ezekiel, and he instantly bonded with Anton and Laith. One of my favorite photos of all time is from after dinner the day he came home. We all went for a walk to show him the neighborhood, the boys wanting to point out to their new sibling the deer we'd often come upon. We lived a handful of blocks from a Boy Scout camp, where at least a hundred Bambi look-alikes roamed the grounds. Ezekiel walked between his little brothers, an arm protectively over each of their shoulders. He barely knew these kids, but he'd already claimed them as his own. Precious.

But the transition wasn't always so idyllic. Bringing a young child from rural Ethiopia to America is like transplanting someone from the eighteenth century into the modern day. He'd never seen an escalator or an elevator, both of which completely confused him. To him, anything electronic was like something from an alien planet. And since Ethiopians eat with their hands, our sweet six-year-old didn't know how to eat with a fork, knife, or spoon.

All experiences were novel for him. A lot were hilarious to watch him figure out, and it was always amazing to see a child learn things before your eyes.

Never having had access to more than a spigot to wash in, the concept of a shower thrilled Ezekiel. I laughed as we listened to him sing familiar songs from my childhood that he'd learned at the orphanage at the top of his lungs in thickly accented English. The china in the cabinets shook at the heavy *thump* of his feet as he danced and marched to songs like "I'm in the Lord's Army (Yes, Sir!)" while giddily splashing around under the warm water.

One morning Ezekiel was showering upstairs as I bathed the younger boys on the first floor. We lived in an older house, whose pipes would creak loudly when both tubs were used at the same time. Suddenly I heard a bloodcurdling scream, the kind no parent expects to hear from their child's lips. One that stops you cold. I bolted upstairs so fast I don't even remember how I got there.

As I pulled back the curtain, there crouched Ezekiel in the far corner of the shower, slinking into the tile. Grasping his knees to his chest and rocking back and forth as the shower sprayed his crumpled figure, he looked at me with eyes as big as saucers, almost animal-like noises of terror coming from his small frame. Fear was written on him from head to toe.

I picked up my little boy, whom I still barely knew, and sat on my bed, wrapping a thick, warm towel tightly around his slim body and swaying him in my arms. *What on earth . . . ?* I thought to myself. I prayed as I spoke quietly to my son, trying to calm him as he shook violently, gulping terrified sobs and struggling to communicate.

Finally, he raised his hands into a gun shape and made machine-gun sounds with his mouth. My heart stopped as I realized that yes, those pipes knocking sounded extremely similar to the sound of a machine gun. Oh, my sweet love. He laid his head on my shoulder as I drew him even closer and cooed gentle encouragement to his scarred heart. I prayed like crazy as my own heart broke that he knew what that sound was. My new son knows the sound of gunfire. And he knows enough of it that it completely terrifies him. Oh Lord, what he's seen and experienced in his short life.

Ezekiel's memories, both real and imagined, resulted in fits as fear came randomly. In the in-between times, though, Ben and I loved seeing his joyful spirit as he gleefully enjoyed Anton, Laith, and baby Imani. His laughter was contagious, and it was easy to smile just being in the same room with him.

But then, about three months into Ezekiel's new life with us, grief and extreme struggle set in. Sadly, San Antonio didn't have so much as an Ethiopian restaurant, so he was thrown into American life without many reminders of home. Ben often brought our favorite Ethiopian dishes home when he had meetings in Austin, thinking an African feast would be a fun treat for our homesick little boy. But he wouldn't eat it. We reached out to a friend of my mother, who is from Eritrea and speaks Amharic, one of the languages Ezekiel speaks. But he wouldn't converse with her. Inadequacy sparked as I fell to my knees asking God how to help him through it all. Fear of failing him, fear of failing as his mom, blazed through me like a quickly spreading wildfire.

We finally concluded someone must have told him not to speak Amharic or to embrace any of his heritage after moving to America, thinking perhaps it would upset us. We've since learned some kids are told if they do, they could be sent back. Perhaps, we thought, he feared if he embraced elements from his old life, he wouldn't be welcomed into his new.

I have been like little Ezekiel. I have hidden the true me, sharing only bits and pieces for fear I wouldn't be wholly embraced. So often I am gripped with fear at the idea that I'll be rejected, that I'm not enough: smart enough, pretty enough, or talented enough. I push away taunting whispers that I'm not a good enough mom, wife, or friend—the list goes on and on. I'm sure I'm not alone, that I'm not the only one who has fears that usher themselves in because of deep shame and a panic that people may find out what we've done, how we've behaved, or what was done to us.

If we don't rest in the truth of Christ and remember that His perfect love casts out fear, this foreboding and shame roots itself deeply into our hearts. Winding its way around, cinching tighter and tighter, we not only begin to live *in* that fear, but it quickly consumes us, forcing us to live in a false identity that no one could love us if they knew who we really are. The whole us, we conclude, isn't someone who could be fully embraced. Fully loved.

The single goal of Satan is for us to forget not just who we are but *whose* we are. He constantly places fear, shame, and guilt on our shoulders like a heavy quilt, pretending to keep us warm, each block of fabric yet another example of why we'll never be enough.

What our sweet son would learn is we love him because he is Ezekiel, not because he is perfect. We love him for his past, we love him for who he is now, and we love him for who the Lord will grow him to be in the future. My eyes are opened to the fact that if I love my family in spite of all their flaws, how much more does Christ love me in spite of mine? He is a God full of grace and mercy. His love is a gift that none of us earns. He loves us because it's in His very nature to love.

"Give your entire attention to what God is doing right now,
and don't get worked up about what
may or may not happen tomorrow.
God will help you deal with whatever hard things
come up when the time comes."
Matthew 6:34 MSG

Shortly after Laith was born, I began having a strange feeling that we wouldn't have him for long. Pushing the horrible idea from my thoughts, I ignored it, mentally cataloguing it as hormonal postpartum delusions. Over and over through the years, the premonition strikes, and with it comes an irrational feeling that his life will be cut short. It's strange at what points my ears tune in to the whisper that something is going to happen to our youngest blondie. It's not when he's skiing fearlessly down the Colorado mountains, nor is it when Ben has taken him on dirt-biking weekends. It's not when he has been so ill his temperature spiked to an unnerving number. Instead, it's random moments and for seemingly no reason.

This child, whom we long ago nicknamed Crazy Crash, as I mentioned earlier, because of his ability to fall onto his head merely walking across the living room to the kitchen, is constantly full of bruises and cuts. He has broken his arm after falling from monkey bars and had to have a rod placed inside, which caused atrophy to set in and required months of physical therapy to make the now-healed arm strong again. He has split open his head, torn a tendon in his leg after jumping off his brother's head (I can't even begin to explain) requiring he wear a boot for many weeks, and been in the hospital for a plethora of other things. After one of his surgeries, a nurse pulled me aside, saying, "God forbid that boy ever gets cancer, but if he did, he'd change the world while beating it."

Who says that to a mom who is walking, keys in hand, to pull the car around to the front of Children's Hospital while her pre-schooler sits in a wheelchair, still fluttering in and out of sleep from anesthesia? Fear seized me when people would say things like this, which, when it came to Laith, was strangely often.

Laith is our sensitive, spiritual one, the kid who taught himself to read before kindergarten so he could read the Bible on his own. He's the one who teaches me Bible verses and asks me theological questions on the drive to school.

This past summer we had family photos taken at sunset, on a mountaintop near our home. At the end of our shoot, the photographer asked Laith to sit on a boulder overlooking the most beautiful forest clearing, the last rays of light streaking down through moody gray-blue clouds. Motioning that I join my sweet son for a picture, I thought she was testing out the shot and lighting and would ask the rest of the family to join us. As she called, "That's a wrap!" and we jumped down, she put her arm around Laith and said, "I can tell you and your mom have a special relationship. She's especially going to want those someday."

What do you meeeaaan?! I wanted to scream into her face and shake an explanation out of her. My heart ached as either lies or truth—I couldn't tell which—swelled through me, thinking there must be a connection with this moment and my young son breathing his last breath. *What is this, Lord? Is it merely a spirit of fear coming to torment me, or is this truly You preparing me for what seems to be a mother's worst nightmare?*

After internally shrieking in horror of what might be, I hoped to hear a murmured reply from God. Instead, I only heard silence. Of this strange premonition, I still have no answers, aside from the knowledge I need to hold everyone in my life loosely. This does not mean I love them any less fiercely, but that I love them *well* and with the knowledge that they perceive both my intensely profound love and our heavenly Father's. He has a plan for Laith's life just as He does for mine. For now, I choose to let this complex worry serve as a reminder to love God more than my children and to get to a place where I could begin to understand the story of Abraham and Isaac. I choose for it to be a constant reminder that I am an instrument to teach my children how to live an openhanded life, so whether Laith reaches eighty or eighteen, his life will be used for the glory of God.

Every morning before our kids walk out the front door to school, I put my arms around them and pray over each of them. It's partly because I want to instill a life of prayer into our children, helping each understand we should commune with our Lord throughout the day and at all times. But I also do it because every single day I have to consciously give them back over to God. These bright-eyed cuties are mine to take care of for now, to grow and nurture and love. But they are actually God's children, and sometimes I hold on to them so tightly that the idea of anything happening to them is too much to bear. Whenever I pray, I try to use the word *our* rather than *my. Lord, thank You for* our *sweet Imani.* It helps me realign myself with the knowledge that they do not belong to me. They are both mine and the Lord's to love and care for. I need to live an openhanded life, conscious that, yes, I love my children—but if *my* heart is about to burst with love for them, think how much greater the Lord's love is for them.

When I was young, a girl in my class was kidnapped on her walk to school. I remember the day like it was yesterday instead of thirty years ago. Because of that day, I have panicked thoughts every time my phone rings on a school morning. *It's the elementary school saying they never made it,* I immediately think as my hand shakes while answering. We live about two hundred yards from the path that enters the school grounds and they never walk alone, always with friends and neighbors. But even so, I worry about them every day. Fear that a shooter will enter their campus haunts me many days as well, especially when driving past Columbine High School. I had just graduated high school myself when that horror occurred, and though I lived in a different part of the country and watched it all on television, we now live a handful of miles away. Each time I drive by I'm haunted by the reality that families have experienced the terror I only see in my mind's eye.

Ezekiel and I were locked up in fear, but faith was the key that let us out. Remembering the story in Mark 9 of the father who brought his son, tormented by an evil spirit, before Jesus to be healed, I brought my son before Him too. In the story, Jesus encouraged the man, saying, "'All things are possible for one who believes.' Immediately the father of the child cried out and said, 'I believe; help my unbelief!'" (Mark 9:23-24 ESV).

Like the father, I believed and struggled with the conviction that things really would get better. I knew God healed, yet my mind struggled to believe it would happen for us.

After Jesus healed the boy, the disciples came before the Messiah asking why they couldn't heal him like they'd been able to in the past. Christ shared that "this kind can come out by nothing but prayer and fasting" (Mark 9:29 NKJV).

I've learned that sometimes God does not move until we pray. We see in Scripture that Jesus commands us to call upon Him. Why? Because God has commanded that certain things will only come to pass in response to our prayers. Believing or trusting that He will do something is very different from the actual act of prayer. Armed with this, I prayed and prayed . . . and after that, I prayed some more. There were times when I didn't even know what to say, salty tears dripping from my eyes and down my chin. As I tearfully sat in silence before His throne, the Holy Spirit interceded for me (Romans 8:26). With groans too deep for words, time and time again the Lord helped me get out from under this overwhelming fear that consumed me.

... 🦢 ...

I know the Lord protects. I've experienced it firsthand in tangible ways when my family lived in Guatemala. Every time I tell people about what our family lived through and witnessed while living there during my junior high years, they've got to think I'm making it up.

While we lived in this beautiful, lush, cobblestoned country, guerrilla warfare ran rampant. Many instances we witnessed firsthand. There were several nights when my brother and I would army-crawl in the darkness from our rooms to the other side of our home to my parents' master bedroom as we heard machine-guns fire close by. We sat under a window (where my parents could sneak peeks outside) in complete silence, knowing our "family plan" and seeing before me the measures my amazing dad would go to protect us.

My dad had been in a SWAT team years before, when we lived in California. He knew what to do to protect his family. He taught us to move quietly in the dark, not wanting to alert anyone that the hangar was inhabited. As mortars exploded on base, I remember seeing their bright-orange fire light up the night sky.

Hand-to-hand combat on the front steps of our home. Gunfire. Running. Shouting.

Like I said, I've seen God's hand of protection firsthand. Many times.

But now that I have a family myself, I have something to lose. And the idea of that grips me.

My all-time favorite passage in the Bible is Psalm 91. Flip open your Bible to it if you're ever needing a reminder of God's goodness and protection. I love the imagery that He will cover us with His feathers and under His wings we will find refuge.

And yet even now I struggle. The boys woke early this morning; the snow is thick in the mountains and ski school awaits. They drive away with Ben, and I wave and watch red taillights glow smaller and smaller down our frost-frozen street, then close the door behind me. Praying.

My cousins visited my family in Seattle when I was in high school. Driving through on their way to visit family in California, they stopped for a quick overnight with dinner and fellowship. We laughed; we exchanged stories; we caught up. Oh, such fun.

The next morning after a hot breakfast of Swedish pancakes and milk poured from my grandmother's porcelain cow-shaped pitcher, hugs were tight all around and again taillights faded down the street.

That was the last time I saw her alive, my sweet cousin, my same age.

A few hours into their drive toward the Golden State and their grandparents' open arms, a man—still drunk from the night before—changed the family forever. Her brothers, her sister, her mother, all scarred inside and out, hearts still aching all these years later, at the loss of a young life.

When will I experience such evil? When will something horrible happen to my innocent children? To my family? I thought as fears coursed through me.

It was never *if*. My mind only blared *when?*

I turned off all news. I no longer turned my knob to the talk radio station I enjoyed in the car. Information of the world around me came to a screeching halt. I couldn't handle it. My heart couldn't handle it. Dreams were dark; fears and situations flashed in my mind's eye during the light of day.

Fear. Such overwhelming fear.

Once again, the Lord drove me to my knees. I needed to get out from under this overwhelming fear that at times consumed me. I prayed for my own struggles, and I prayed for Ezekiel's. I found strength in the knowledge that we were going through something similar. I could identify with his fears. Though my fear didn't manifest itself in my sleep and was rather my mind's eye thinking the worst of the what-ifs, they were still much the same.

I realized something one day, though. Again, learning from the image of the storm:

> *It's not the absence of the storms that set us apart.*
> *It's whom we discover in the storm: an unstirred Christ.*
> Max Lucado[16]

What is the opposite of faith? Doubt? Skepticism? Distrust? I have come to realize, rather, it is fear.

> *We need have no fear of someone who loves us perfectly;*
> *his perfect love for us eliminates all dread*
> *of what he might do to us. If we are afraid,*
> *it is for fear of what he might do to us and shows*
> *that we are not fully convinced that he really loves us.*
> 1 John 4:18 TLB

As fear sought to dismantle my joy these past few years, I've become more determined to stand strong in my faith in Jesus. I've decided to refuse to live a life that shatters the promises Christ has given me. I've realized I must give it all back to Him, because if I don't, I'll completely unravel. Jesus did not die on the cross so I could live a life of timidity and fear. He came so I may have a life abundant, and in that knowledge, I must place my trust.

When getting up each day, I must make the same decision the disciples made as they got up and followed Him, leaving their old lives behind. If I'm going to be used by God to the fullest, I need to make the conscious decision to be raw, authentic, and bold as I also accept Jesus's invitation to leave the old me behind and become the new creation we learn about in 2 Corinthians 5:17.

Ann Voskamp says, "All fear is but the notion that God's love ends," and there is no doubt in my mind that His doesn't.[17] Ever.

CHAPTER 13

The Widow and the Oil

> *God loves each of us as if there were only one of us.*
>
> ST. AUGUSTINE

After bringing Ezekiel home, things continued changing, and Ben and I soon realized a big move was in our future and we needed once again to pray hard. We'd both felt for a year or more that San Antonio was no longer where the Lord wanted us. We were being released of this city with its River Walk, Mexican food, loving friends, and where my family had followed us.

As I mentioned earlier, after deciding he wanted to be where his nephew was, my brother, Erik, had transported his life in Washington and moved in with us the week Anton was born. Then came baby Laith. Meanwhile, Erik met the most incredible girl whom he (so wisely) married, and they became a family. My grandmother also moved to the heat of San Antonio, followed by my parents.

How could we leave a family that had moved across the country to be closer to us and our children? How would we listen to God when once again He didn't make sense? My family had all uprooted their lives to be with us in Texas, and though we told them we didn't think we'd be in San Antonio forever, at the same time, once it became real, it was scary. And more than a little sad to start all over again.

But Colorado became our future. Specifically, Denver. God was exceedingly clear about it.

Conversations were had. Tears flowed. And boxes were packed. With a heavy heart about who we left behind, my soul soared knowing we were listening to the voice of our Father in heaven, knowing He had been preparing our family for this new adventure.

When I was a child and our family prepared to move to Guatemala, we spent a few days at Disneyland with my grandparents who wintered in California. I remember so clearly them hugging us good-bye, eyes willing away the tears and forcing smiles, trying to be brave.

Those days flashed before me, and I knew that just as my parents were called away from what was comfortable, so were we. We opened our hands to release all we desired to hold tightly, allowing the Lord to work in our lives, to direct us to where He wanted us to go.

It's hard. It's scary. And sometimes it's as painful as it is exciting. But this is the life we want: Unordinary. One where our ears are in tune to Him. One where He asks and we answer. Or really, *we* ask and *He* answers.

Ben crossed the state lines in my car, accompanied by our chocolate lab, Thatcher, and my folks drove Ben's truck. I flew alone with all four kids. *Thank You, Jesus, that this is a direct flight*, I silently prayed as I searched for dollar bills in my wallet, preoccupying our giddy children with snacks and chocolate milk as we waited for our plane.

God was gracious that day. It went smooth as silk. The Crazies (which we lovingly call our kids), though buzzed with this new adventure, settled nicely into their seats, playing quietly together and giggling sweetly as turbulence jostled their little tummies. We stood together at baggage claim, eyes searching for our oversized luggage. Tears came to my eyes as I thanked Him for His goodness.

Bags in tow, I stopped at the nearby Starbucks for a (much needed) latte. The barista smiled at me traveling alone with my brood of small children, and as we chatted lightly, I asked if he was from Ethiopia. The twinkle in his eye as he looked at me in surprise told me he was. The kids, making a flaky mess on the floor with their croissants, waited for me with surprising contentment as my new barista friend told me I'd just moved to a city with one of the largest Ethiopian communities in the entire country.

"What?" I breathlessly asked him.

He laughed as he told me that if Ethiopians took a strike, the entire airport would shut down. "We run the place," he told me, that twinkle still in his eye.

He told me about all the Ethiopian restaurants, Ethiopian markets, Ethiopian churches, and on and on.

Oh Lord God, You answer prayers I didn't even think to pray.

We went from a city with not a single Ethiopian restaurant to one with thousands upon thousands of people with our children's heritage. I was speechless, a lump in my throat growing as I silently praised our heavenly Father.

Oh Father, thank You for opening our hearts to listen to You and where You wanted us to go. Let us always follow Your leading, for You will take abundantly better care of us than we could take of ourselves.

God knew we couldn't go with Him *and* stay where we were. Christ knew, far before we would, that the Ethiopian community in Denver would be like a lifeline for our family.

It had been a few years since Imani and Ezekiel came home, and since we moved from San Antonio to Denver. Though we felt fairly settled with our expanded family, we still waded through hurts and fears, trauma and loss. We were in the middle of completely remodeling a home we had recently bought that was deemed "uninhabitable." We had rented a house, sight unseen via Craigslist, before moving to the Rocky Mountain state, and we unpacked as little as possible knowing we needed to search out this beautiful land, not knowing where within its borders we should ultimately spread roots. When we finally moved to a house of our own, we were excited about the idea of this rundown and unlivable house.

Once again, friends and family thought we were crazy as we shared that the home we had purchased in our new city was falling apart at the seams. Shoddy construction and second-rate updating barely held a candle to the devastation the home withstood after its previous owners took out their anger on the kitchen and other spaces when told their home was no longer theirs, somehow blind to the fact this was inevitable after many months of not paying their mortgage.

But within the pumpkin-orange sponge-painted walls, crumbling staircase, and dry rot, Ben and I saw potential. We saw what *could* be. We love tearing down walls and building things back up. This would be our sixth house in about as many years. These projects of perseverance and creativity, of breathing life into what had previously been unsightly or dirty and distasteful brought us extreme joy.

I am an aesthetic kind of girl. I have a deep affection for all five senses and love to add a little romance into life. I don't mean necessarily with a beau, but with life in general. I'm the kind of girl who watches a movie with candles lit and cooks while listening to the Andrea Bocelli channel on Pandora. I buy flowers from the grocery store on a weekly basis, arranging them in vintage cups and placing them throughout the house, knowing somehow these little acts of appreciating beauty bring me closer in relationship with God because they fill my heart. I've realized through the years that a home doesn't have to be perfect to be beautiful, and remind myself of it often as I pour through my favorite design books again and again. Just like our scars, houses often bear character from the past and embracing it brings a uniqueness we wouldn't otherwise have.

I think God was using this house to show us He was going to do the same within our hearts, and this love of refurbishing our home became a metaphor for what He was doing to us and our family. He would continue to tear down expectations and plans, building up something better and more beautiful.

The building and remodeling process of homes had always brought Ben and me together, and the building of our family (though certainly tough at times) brought a strength between Ben and me that we didn't know we had. Apparently we had learned how to use stress to better our marriage. Can you hear me laughing at that statement?

We know now that learning to lean on Christ first and each other second was in preparation for bringing another child with hurts and fears and a life of tragedy into our family. We knew we'd never feel fully prepared, fully groomed for this calling. And yet, here we were. A few short years of experience tucked into our belts, we readied for more mess in construction and the challenge of erecting a solid family, reinforced in the strength of a most gracious heavenly Father.

We had saved our pennies when contemplating the adoptions of Imani and Ezekiel. We'd known for many months that our hearts were being tugged in that direction before accepting either referral. We'd had time to save.

But Abreham's story came out of the blue; our knowing he was our son was unexpected.

It was a typical midweek afternoon. Lunch had been enjoyed, and the kitchen was momentarily clean, rid of the ever-constant stream of dishes and crumbs that seemed a permanent fixture on our countertops. I had cozied into the couch with a gloriously hot cup of coffee for a few moments of brainless me time. As I scrolled first through Pinterest, then through Facebook, I paused. Breathless.

A fellow adoptive mom had posted a story about a teenaged boy from Ethiopia who was in need of a family. I read and reread the words she had typed into her feed and read them again as my heart beat out of my chest.

This is my son.

Lord, I think this is my son. Why do I think that? Is he ours? This does not make sense. No. He's a teenager! What?! No, Lord. No—I'm not telling YOU no—I'm just saying, well . . . THIS IS MY SON, isn't it?

I went back and forth, half-arguing but mostly putting up a pretend fight with the Lord, mind blown at the sudden change in direction our life had taken in a split second. I felt as strongly as I'd ever felt anything in my entire life, that this boy named Abreham was mine. And I was his.

Me, the non-crier, cried on and off most of the rest of the afternoon in acknowledgment that my son lived in an orphanage. And we needed to get him home.

As the afternoon bled into evening and Ben walked through the door from work, the kitchen no longer bore any signs of having been briefly spotless. Instead, the makings of dinner were spread across the gray countertops. Crayons, coloring books, and small children sprawled out on the wooden floor behind me. The kids, suddenly on their feet with squeals of "Daddy's home!" interrupted Ben's stride to give me a kiss hello while I stirred dinner on the stove.

When the little ones finally had their fill of kisses, hugs, and giggles from tickle fights, my happy yet tired husband came my way. As he neared, knowing it's my favorite, he kissed me on the forehead, and said with resolution in his voice, "We need to chat."

Quickly and without hesitation, I verbally spewed, "Is it about a boy named Abreham? Because I think he's our son."

Ben paused and stared at me, his eyes momentarily growing wide. Then as a smile slowly spread across his face, we knew God was at work again. Ben had seen Abreham's story on social media that same day. Different social media outlet, different person posting, but the same message that this boy needed a family. And the Lord had opened my husband's heart wide throughout the rest of the day, just as He had mine.

Head swirling and randomly giggling at the insanity of it all, we joined God in what He was asking of us.

Several months later, after Christmas ornaments were snugly packed away and daffodils and tulips took their place, our heavenly Father would rock our boat once again.

As we ushered our children out of church on Easter morning and toward the car, the boys clad in matching seersucker shorts and Imani donning lace socks and a frilly frock, I helped buckle in those who still struggled to do it without help. As Ben climbed in, waiting patiently for me to click my own seat belt into place, he checked the e-mail on his phone. Seeing the director of our agency's name in his in-box, he opened up the message, expecting to find a short update on Abreham or even some new photos of our oldest son. What he found instead was a string of a dozen or so photos of a tiny infant girl, the last few of Abreham holding the little girl. As I turned to Ben, wondering why we had yet to drive out of the quickly emptying lot full of hungry families headed to brunch and egg hunts, he handed me his phone, tears beginning to spring up into his eyes.

Confused, especially at the sight of his damp eyes, I took hold of the phone he held out and saw her beautiful face staring back at me. I scrolled past the awkward photos of Abreham and this little girl both wearing ridiculous plush bunny ears and the one of her face red and scrunched up in the middle of a wail. I scrolled slowly past the one of her staring contently with eyes as dark as night, noticing right away that her tummy bore no evidence of malnutrition and looked perfect and healthy. As I continued scrolling and scrolling, my mind continuing to scream, *Who is this?* and *Could she be mine?* Finally, I paused on one of the last photos, stopping to peer at Abreham's face as he held her. His hands looked clumsy, as if he wasn't yet used to holding an infant. But his eyes bore truth in the joy of doing so.

I looked at Ben. "Who is this girl?" I could barely murmur.

Grinning like the Cheshire Cat, he urged me to read the e-mail.

"This is your daughter," it read. There was more, of course. About how it was our turn on the infant waiting list and that they had already told Abreham this was his sister because they knew we would say yes. But all I could read and reread were those words: *This is your daughter.*

We'd had a surprise pregnancy with Anton. We'd also been a bit taken aback when the Lord unexpectedly revealed His bringing Ezekiel and Abreham into our family. But this. This somehow felt different. Like the biggest and most unexpected surprise of my life.

I genuinely don't remember putting ourselves back on the infant waiting list. Ben says we did, so how I don't remember confuses me even still. I think maybe back when I was swaying back and forth, praying and pondering for God's discernment and wisdom in the growth of our family, He made the decision for me. Instead of giving me the responsibility of figuring out His will in becoming pregnant or adopting an infant, the Lord prompted Ben to contact our agency and somehow allowed me to have blinders regarding it.

Our newest and youngest child, Milki, was soon to be ours. Like Imani, her name didn't hold much significance, it was given to her at the orphanage. We searched and searched for the origin meanings of her name, and found that Elsabet was of Hebrew origin (the equivalent of Elizabeth in English). When we shared the news of our family gaining another sibling, Ezekiel asked if we could name her Hannah, after his dearly missed older sister, who still lives in Ethiopia. So she became Elsabet Hannah Anderson.

This gift of another baby girl was more than I could ever hope for or imagine. Imani would have a sister. I would once again be blessed with the gift of having someone fall asleep on my chest. This time, somehow unlike the others, I looked forward to the idea of being coated in spit up, looking frazzled and unkempt from sleepless nights. This felt right and whole and big. I will never forget that Easter, never forget bursting into irrational laughter, like a madwoman, in the middle of serving eggs Benedict and lemonade.

Mind still swirling gleefully days later, a sobering thought took hold: *How are we going to pay for all this?*

While sitting down with the Lord during my quiet time one morning, I felt Him prompt me to read in the book of 2 Kings. I recognized that if God wanted these children to join our family, somehow He would make it happen. Clenching my eyes tight in prayer, I brought my tiny sliver of trust before Him. A part of me knew He would bring it all together, just as He had before. But at the same time, my so-called rational mind glimpsed at the uncertainty of it all as doubts of, *But what if He doesn't come through this time?* buzzed in my mind.

Leafing through my Bible searching for the passage, I quickly realized there was a big learning opportunity for me in regard to how much I trusted Him with something as cliché sounding as our finances. Our heavenly Father reminded my weak faith that He would care for our family just as He had for the dear widow in 2 Kings.

One day the widow of a member of the group of prophets came to Elisha and cried out, "My husband who served you is dead, and you know how he feared the LORD. But now a creditor has come, threatening to take my two sons as slaves."

"What can I do to help you?" Elisha asked. "Tell me, what do you have in the house?"

"Nothing at all, except a flask of olive oil," she replied.

And Elisha said, "Borrow as many empty jars as you can from your friends and neighbors. Then go into your house with your sons and shut the door behind you. Pour olive oil from your flask into the jars, setting each one aside when it is filled."

So she did as she was told. Her sons kept bringing jars to her, and she filled one after another. Soon every container was full to the brim!

"Bring me another jar," she said to one of her sons.

"There aren't any more!" he told her. And then the olive oil stopped flowing.

When she told the man of God what had happened, he said to her, "Now sell the olive oil and pay your debts, and you and your sons can live on what is left over."

2 Kings 4:1–7 NLT

Reading these words comforted my questioning heart, and as I handed my fears over to the Lord to toss away, He settled my heart that He would stretch our finances. I didn't ask how; I merely felt a certainty about it. Somehow His will would be done; I was simply to move and do what I could while He would do the real work.

As I shared the message I felt God give me while chatting with my mom the following morning, I could hear her smile over the phone as she reminded me, "What is money to God, anyway?"

God sent us on yet another adventure of faith. We applied for grants, petitioned for endowments. But we weren't to receive any.

Let us then approach God's throne of grace with confidence,
so that we may receive mercy and find grace
to help us in our time of need.
Hebrews 4:16 NIV

We began an online fund-raiser through an amazing 501(c)(3), where friends, family, and generous people we had never even met began to give $5, $10, $50, and some even donated thousands. The money began adding up, at first incredibly slowly, then the speed of it all began to pick up.

But if He calls you to something, have faith He will see it to fulfillment. Even if it makes absolutely no sense to you how it possibly will.

My sweet cousin Katherine began an auction through Facebook. Sharing our story, she asked acquaintances and even merchants on Etsy to donate items. Again, every little bit helped.

Ben's youngest sister wanted to contribute but was still in college and didn't have much to donate. Thinking outside the box, Sara decided to have a house party. Sharing our story with her friends, a donation jar was passed through the rooms and with a few crumpled dollars here and crisp, just-out-of-the-ATM dollars there, we were astonished by the number she ended up contributing. College kids eating ramen and saving their quarters for the laundromat ended up being a big reason our children are home with us today.

Our new home had no kitchen, walls had been ripped out to the studs, and the stairs were being replaced because they were so wobbly and dangerous. The list of our home's projects went on and on, and our resources were already stretched thinner than normal.

How the Lord worked it all out, I have no idea.

But if He calls you to something, have faith He will see it to fulfillment. Even if it makes absolutely no sense to you how it possibly will.

And we know that in all things
God works for the good of those who love him,
who have been called according to his purpose.
Romans 8:28 NIV

And as always, God was orchestrating things to work in His good and perfect timing. It looked like we would be able to bring our children home together.

And my God will meet all your needs according
to the riches of his glory in Christ Jesus.
Philippians 4:19 NIV

School let out, and soon weeks, then months passed. Once again we became discouraged, knowing the rainy season was quickly approaching. Changes and rumors of changes for adoptions in Ethiopia began to emerge. We were getting nervous that we would have to wait until mid- to late fall to bring them home.

I began, once again, to pray very specifically for the timing of our children's arrival to the US. I felt a deep importance in getting Abreham home before the school year began. Ideally, we wanted him to be with us for a handful of weeks to settle in and begin to bond with the family before the whirlwind and overwhelming task of school began. We also desired that our new son have a few English words in his vocabulary.

Again, I prayed fervently, I prayed specifically, and I prayed in faith that the Lord was listening as I laid my requests at His feet, and laid my fears and worries alongside them.

Do not be anxious about anything,
but in every situation,
by prayer and petition, with thanksgiving,
present your requests to God.
Philippians 4:6 NIV

For months leading up to when we hoped we'd be able to travel for our Ethiopian court date, Anton, then six years old, asked if he could join us. We gathered the children together one evening and asked if everyone wanted to come. Ezekiel had no desire. We've always said when he turns sixteen, we will take the family and try to find his mother and sister. He said that was what he still wanted, but he wasn't ready to go back yet. We felt Laith (not quite five) and Imani (nearly three) would be hard to travel with when all attention needed to be on the newest two children. They didn't particularly care to come anyway. I think they liked the idea of staying with Grandma while we were gone.

So we sat Anton down and had an honest and grown-up conversation with him, explaining what it was like, what he'd see. We talked about how important it was for this trip to be about his newest siblings and to help them feel loved by us. We spoke of the length of the plane ride and the lack of American food.

He understood. And he was in.

Finally, we received "the call." We were to leave in a few days and looked forward to Skyping with Abreham that Saturday and telling him about our trip. He seemed thrilled, as he now expertly held baby Elsabet to the computer's camera so we could see her better.

We all smiled and laughed lamely through the screen, wishing we could understand each other more, Ben and I aching to bring them both home.

During that conversation, we were told the orphanage was out of formula for the babies. We were stunned. They rely heavily on families who come in for their court or embassy dates to bring formula, diapers, etc., with them, and because of changes in the country and the adoption process slowing down, less families had come through, and the abundance of these necessary items had also slowed. I was panicked, remembering how malnourished Imani had been when we brought her home, and I refused to allow that to happen to any more babies (if I had anything to say about it). We are big advocates for purchasing needed items in-country, to wrap our arms around individuals working so hard to provide for their families. If we can help the economy, even in the tiniest of ways, we always strive to do that. In this situation however, the nannies were very specific in what they asked for. They knew the brands of items they wanted because they desired specific nutrients for these babies in their care.

With that in mind, we told friends through Facebook and e-mail that we were only bringing carry-ons for ourselves and had purchased six of the largest suitcases we could find at Goodwill to load full of formula, clothing, diapers, and anything else we could get our hands on for the children who had spent the past months with ours.

We were PayPaled money, checks came in the mail, and an abundance of cans were dropped without notes at our doorstep. I'm choking back tears typing this, remembering the generosity of those in our community and throughout the nation who stepped up for those who couldn't help themselves.

Pure and genuine religion in the sight of God the Father
means caring for orphans and widows in their distress
and refusing to let the world corrupt you.
James 1:27 NLT

The community around us acted as the hands and feet of Jesus. And because of that, bellies would be full. Funding for our adoptions was like the widow's oil, and so was the amount of formula donated. We squeezed every last canister into the suitcases. With no room to spare.

> *Do not think that love, in order to be genuine,*
> *has to be extraordinary.*
> *What we need is to love without getting tired.*
> Mother Teresa

Knowing God had so obviously orchestrated our family coming together as one, Ben, Anton, and I sat giddy while bumping along over potholes and dirt roads, taking what seemed like forever to get to the orphanage and to our children. We pulled into the orphanage and as we parked, I noticed Abreham shyly waiting for us just inside the gate as other children rushed down to greet us. It was awkward for a moment as he held out his hand for me to shake it. "Shake your hand?" I laughed. "Child, you're my *son*," I said quietly in his ear as I hugged him close. I knew he didn't understand my words, but there was no doubt he could sense our elation and love for him.

After a round of nervous hugs, Abreham took us upstairs to meet baby Elsabet. On our way up the stairs and through the beautiful mansion turned orphanage, Abreham stopped us briefly to show us his drawings. He had turned many of the scenes from photos we'd sent of our family and life in the US into brightly colored pieces of art on scraps of paper. He was so proud of the work he'd done and grinned from ear to ear while pressing them all into our hands, obvious gifts from his heart.

Continuing on to the nursery where Elsabet was, I melted into her tiny frame as her nanny placed my daughter into my arms. She was so perfect and beautiful. Her tummy was flat and healthy, show-ing no signs of being malnourished like Imani. I shot up a quick, yet emphatic prayer of praise.

Spending the week together was amazing. We frequented the market, restaurants, the museum to see the famous fossilized bones of Lucy, drove around sightseeing, and discovered a favorite donut place and a street vendor who made the most wonderful lentil and meat filled samosas.

Ben and I swayed back and forth trying to decide whether I would just stay in Ethiopia for the few weeks between our court trip and when the US Embassy completed the paperwork, granting our children permission to come home. Ultimately, though, I knew I needed to come home, the children needing me since Ben was unable to take the several weeks off from work and we didn't have family in-state. I mourned leaving Abreham and Elsabet, just as I'd mourned coming home after being with Imani and Ezekiel. At least, I tried to console myself, I knew they were being well-loved and cared for at the transition house in our absence.

Days and weeks passed, and finally we got word that I possi-bly had an Embassy appointment. In and out of sleep that night, I groggily listened to the light tapping of Ben on his laptop. Cuddling closer to him as I squinted at the clock on my bedside table, I saw it read 2:00 a.m., then it was 4:00 a.m. and he was still typing away. As the sun just began to peek into our windows, I felt a nudge and a hug while dazedly trying to figure out what was going on.

"You're going *tonight!*" he excitedly whispered in my ear.

I bolted up. "*What?!* The embassy finally e-mailed you?"

Since Ethiopia is ten hours ahead of us in Colorado, my sweet husband had stayed up all night, anticipating the embassy's confir-mation e-mail to come through. Meanwhile, all through the night, he worked on our side with a travel agency, trying for all his worth to get me on a plane that evening and back home four days later. Plane tickets were skyrocketing and it was looking like our tickets would be thousands of dollars more than we could ever afford. With literally ten or more hours of searching flights, talking with different travel agencies, and *tons* of prayer, Ben was able to somehow acquire our tickets for several thousand less. Thank You, Lord.

I vividly remember standing near the snack shack at our neighborhood pool talking to a few friends while the kids splashed at swimming lessons, mere hours after I had packed my carry-on and slid a couple prepared meals in the fridge. I couldn't stop shaking, the excitement and adrenaline taking over. We were *so* ready to get Abreham and Elsabet home, yet still not totally ready at the same time. The whole day we were switching beds around to fit the right number of beds in various bedrooms, finally configuring it so everyone fit: two kids in each tiny room. While standing at the pool, I realized I needed to release my hopes of having every detail perfect and complete like I had obsessed about when Ezekiel came home. Abreham and Ezekiel's new room had gone from lavender to a pale army green, but remained empty, paint-speckled drop cloths still on the ground awaiting one last coat of paint. I was thankful once again to have an incredible husband who was willing to check off the silly-yet-important-to-me things that remained on my to-do list. Things like putting up drapes, pictures, and moving the boy's furniture back in.

My time in Ethiopia raced by. I was on the ground for thirty-six hours before boarding a plane with a five-month-old infant and a nearly fourteen-year-old boy who spoke no English. I remember our lawyer, Dereje, coming sit with Abreham and me in the living room of the guesthouse I was staying in. I asked Dereje to translate a few details to Abreham about what this trip would be like. I told him what an airplane ride was like, how the turbulence would sometimes shake us but it didn't mean we were about to crash. I also described, and this was very important, what it meant to have a connecting flight. I was terrified about losing him between flights while I stopped into a bathroom to change Elsabet's diaper or use the facilities myself. I made sure he understood it was imperative to stand right outside the bathroom and to not walk away.

The flights were long but they went fairly well, though it was definitely an adventure to do it alone. We watched loads of movies and sweet Ethiopian women gleefully took darling little Elsabet here and there so I could get a few moments of sleep. On our final leg of the trip home, I'd randomly burst out with the giggles, recalling Abreham's first ride on an escalator at the airport in Addis Ababa, the two of us watching the video I'd taken of him over and over, shaky though it was because I was laughing so hard while filming it (it was exactly like in the movie *Elf* if you need a good visual).

Finally we landed in Denver and my stomach was in absolute knots.

This was it.

Our lives would forever be changed as our two newest children came into the reality of our every day. The party near baggage claim was epic, though the balloons and signs and whooping and hollering were a little much for Abreham to absorb. He stood there in shock, looking with wide eyes at the many people who had prayed for him months upon months. Clinging to Anton because he was a familiar face, we eventually walked to the car . . . and life was never the same again.

PART FIVE

Living Boldly

CHAPTER 14

See, I Am Doing a New Thing

. . . . 🦢 . . . .

It has always seemed to me that broken things,
just like broken people, get used more;
it's probably because God has more pieces to work with.

BOB GOFF

n the beginning months after bringing each child home, it seemed that every time we finally felt like our family was settling in, they were beginning to comprehend the depth of our love, things suddenly took a drastic and dramatic turn that left Ben and I bewildered.

A few years ago, shortly after one of the routine check-ins with our social worker, Ben received a call from Child Protective Services. A woman was phoning to inform him that his wife (ME!) was being investigated for child abuse and they were coming by our home to interview all the children and open a case against me because of something a child had said during our recent session.

I cannot even begin to explain to you the loss I felt at that moment.

After meeting with a pastor friend at the Ethiopian Evangelical Church nearby to try to understand the thoughts and intent of this child, I drove home alone. Leaving the stereo off, needing the quiet, I talked to God. In pouring my heart out to Him, I felt Him whisper, *Do not fear. I am allowing you to go through this for a reason.* My soul stilled as I absorbed these words.

Do not fear . . . I began to tear up. This is such a good example of my fears. I hold on so tightly to my family. The idea of anyone being taken from us frightens me to my very core. I was reminded of the overwhelming fear that had consumed my heart the past few years, just waiting for my "when." *When* will we experience firsthand the evil in this world?

Well, I supposed this was one of those times.

What will you do with this fear? I felt the Lord ask me. *Will you let it consume you? Or will you trust Me?*

Oh Lord, I can trust You.

What a blessing it is that I have a Helper who knows more than I do. How good my God is, and how glad I am that He is God and I am not. I will not be afraid. I will allow this storm to swirl around, encircling me. Though my hair may whip in the wind, my soul will be still, knowing His supreme protection surrounds me. I may be bent, but I most certainly will not break. I refuse to break—I'll instead hold onto Him white-knuckled.

"The Lord is my helper; I will not be afraid."
Hebrews 13:6 NIV

A few days later, two ladies from the state came to talk with our family. They were pleasant and friendly, and our children enjoyed answering their questions. Not knowing the real reason of this time together, they giggled and cuddled, their sweet and loving personalities shining through brightly. All but our little love who had cried wolf, that is.

By the end of the several-hours-long meeting, our Hurting One began to soften and wanted to speak with one of the women alone. Because I was helping a few of the other kids get out the door so they could ride their bikes to school and not miss the entire day, I didn't hear their conversation. Finally returning from the other room, the woman spoke to me while shrugging into her coat, mentioning that she would return again. "It is obvious," she said, "the child has more to say."

Thanking her for her time, I closed the front door and leaned my head against it. My head throbbed, as did my jaw. I must've been clenching it the entire time. Going over the meeting in my head, I wondered why they were investigating me, yet they barely asked me any questions. Everything was aimed toward the children or Ben, and though he did his best to steer the conversation to me, they didn't seem all that interested in what I had to say. Defending myself at this time wasn't an option.

I hoped they left seeing what Ben and I saw: a happy and thriving family and a wounded child who needed help and love. A child who had experienced so much tragedy and trauma that only now that they lived in safety could they begin to comprehend what it means to trust.

My confidence was in the Lord, and with sweaty palms I reminded myself that I was not going to give in to fear, and thus refused to be afraid of the outcome. There was nothing more I could do and knew praying was the extent of actionable direction I had available. I knew I needed God to step in and do the rest.

This book is many years in the making, so all my thoughts and feelings of this bewildering experience are documented in very raw early drafts. I mention this because it's important to understand I'm not saying things years later with a different disposition. I have been able to see, as I have worked on this book, where my heart was at the time. It's simple to feel one way after the fact, to believe falsely that my faith didn't begin to wobble. I could have blamed God or begun to second-guess having brought this child into our home. But the truth is, my faith didn't wobble and I never wanted to give up on my child. It's only by the strength of God that I could genuinely say, "I understand that at this point I cannot do anything more, and I trust the Lord enough to know that He will somehow bring beauty from ashes, even if my children are taken from my arms."

True, I had nothing to hide, and I prayed this important fact shone through. But my body was exhausted. After the meeting, I fell asleep on our worn leather couch halfway through the day, only to wake to our chocolate lab kissing my cheek. I was weary. My body ached, my stomach was upset, and I didn't feel my joyful self. I felt beat-up—body, soul, and mind.

Our Hurting One came home from school a few hours later,

quiet and disengaged. By the time we had finished dinner as a family, however, our child began to thaw and their sweet self began to emerge once again. Ben took some of our other loves on an ice-skating date, and I was alone with the one-whose-heart-was-in-shambles. Pouring a cup of milk, the Hurting One sat at the table where I was reading and seemed comfortable and at ease. My happy child had returned. And I took advantage of the good mood.

"Would you go get your Bible?" I asked. "Sure!" my lone child for the night responded, grinning at me. Back in a flash, the precious Book held under a thin arm, our child seemed excited that we were going to discuss something to do with the Bible: a favorite topic of conversation. Bible in lap and flipping to 1 Corinthians 13, we read the entire chapter together:

> *If I speak with human eloquence and angelic ecstasy but don't love, I'm nothing but the creaking of a rusty gate.*
>
> *If I speak God's Word with power, revealing all his mysteries and making everything plain as day, and if I have faith that says to a mountain, "Jump," and it jumps, but I don't love, I'm nothing.*
>
> *If I give everything I own to the poor and even go to the stake to be burned as a martyr, but I don't love, I've gotten nowhere. So, no matter what I say, what I believe, and what I do, I'm bankrupt without love.*
>
> *Love never gives up.*
> *Love cares more for others than for self.*
> *Love doesn't want what it doesn't have.*
> *Love doesn't strut,*
> *Doesn't have a swelled head,*
> *Doesn't force itself on others,*
> *Isn't always "me first,"*
> *Doesn't fly off the handle,*

Doesn't keep score of the sins of others,
Doesn't revel when others grovel,
Takes pleasure in the flowering of truth,
Puts up with anything,
Trusts God always,
Always looks for the best,
Never looks back,
But keeps going to the end.

1 Corinthians 13:1–7 MSG

I explained to our sweet child that if they truly wanted to be a follower of Christ who desires to bring others into relationship with Him, love is the most important characteristic we can possess. If we have not love, we are nothing but noise. No one will look at us and want what we have if we treat one another poorly. Especially if we are unloving to family members, to those who are closest and who love us the most.

"You prayed for an education," I continued. "God heard you, and understanding the deep whispers of your heart, He answered by setting you into a family as well. We are the family that He thought was best for you." Our child was just beginning to learn and understand English, so I tried my best to share my heart with them while keeping it simple. I reminded our Hurting One that I knew it wasn't easy . . . everything was new and different, and they were being asked to live with a group of people who they had only just begun to get to know and yet was told we were their family. I wanted this one to understand I knew their heart and mind were in a whirlwind, being in a household with a language they didn't yet speak well and that had idiosyncrasies they had yet to grasp. I concluded with, "But, my sweet, please know we're doing our best and you really can trust us. This is so new for us, just as it is for you. But I can tell you one thing for certain: we love you and won't give up on you. Ever."

Our child's eyes were focused on me while nodding, actively

engaged in what I was saying. There was so much more I wanted to say, but I knew in that season our child could only glean a pinprick of what I desired to breathe into such a hurting heart. I peered into aching eyes that seemed to be taking it in, letting both my and the Lord's words sink into the deepest parts of their soul.

All I could do was silently petition the Holy Spirit to use words I could not and that our Hurting One would be willing to let us in. That day or someday.

It took us a while, but we realized later that our Hurting One didn't hate me as this made-up story whirled around us like a bad dream. Our child believed if things became hard enough for us that we'd put them back on a plane to Ethiopia.

It makes me so angry when people congratulate us for "saving a child," saying "they must be so much happier in the US."

"No!" I want to yell in their faces. "You have no idea what you're saying, how difficult it is to bring a child from one culture to another. There is no better, there is only different." Life in Ethiopia may have its struggles, but it is an incredible country with so much joy and beauty, whose people have strength and perseverance we can barely fathom.

When Moses led the Israelites out of Egypt and into the wilderness, they didn't feel "saved" every moment of the day. Life was difficult and it was different. At one point, there was grumbling over the type of food the Lord had provided for them to eat that some actually regretting leaving slavery, saying, "At least we enjoyed meat." (Exodus 16).

It's so easy to forget hardship once we're out and on the other side of it. It doesn't mean we're completely void of difficulty; it simply means we have come into a different type of struggle. Our child no longer slept on the streets in a home made from discarded wood and metal. Yet in *that* life, they understood their lot. In that life, they might have been on a lower rung of society, but at least they knew what that looked like. In that life, our Hurting One knew where they belonged. In this new life with this new family, everything was so confusing that they didn't feel they belonged anywhere.

The language was different, the food tasted strange, sights, smells, experiences—everything was new and unfamiliar. Our little love was just like the Israelites who were taken out of captivity, and like them, sometimes it felt easier to go back.

How are we not just the same? When have we taken a leap, suddenly finding ourselves in unfamiliar territory? Motherhood, for example. You want children, pray and pray to become pregnant or to adopt . . . and then *screeeeech!* Chaos and exhaustion rumble over your life as you wonder what you got yourself into.

Or perhaps your little side job became a full-time gig and you think all your dreams have come true as your entrepreneurial venture soars with success. Yet shortly after, reality crashes in with the realization that it's difficult. As all the extra hours pile upon your shoulders in an attempt to keep up, you wonder if it would had been easier to simply stay small where you were.

Everyone with a passion or calling will feel this way at one point or another. The important thing to understand is what to do with this feeling. Do we push through on our own? Do we become depressed and fearful? Or do we cling desperately to Christ through the struggle, praying that somehow there's Purpose with a big capital *P* behind it?

Friends asked if I was angry with this child. Simply put, no. Not for a minute. Rather than anger, sadness was all I felt, that and the knowledge that God was in charge and He knew the end of our story. All I could do was continue to pray for my Hurting One and trust that God would open this wounded heart to the gift of family.

I stood determined and put a stake in the ground convincing myself over and over that I would *not* let fear grasp me.

Around this time, Ben flew out of town, and I was faced with dressing up six kids and driving them to church alone. Knowing I needed someone to spoon-feed life and wisdom into me, I tossed breakfast dishes into the dishwasher with relief in my eyes. Church is my second home. I haven't always felt this way—sometimes Starbucks felt like they doled out more joy than sitting in a pew ever could— and yet I thanked Jesus as I buttoned those little shirts and tied those dirty laces because these words in 1 Peter seemed meant for me:

> *Who is going to harm you if you are eager to do good?*
> *But even if you should suffer for what is right, you are blessed.*
> *"Do not fear their threats; do not be frightened." But in your*
> *hearts revere Christ as Lord. Always be prepared to give*
> *an answer to everyone who asks you to give the reason for*
> *the hope that you have. But do this with gentleness*
> *and respect, keeping a clear conscience, so that those*
> *who speak maliciously against your good behavior*
> *in Christ may be ashamed of their slander.*
> 1 Peter 3:13–16 NIV

Sitting at the very back of the sanctuary, allowing myself to be alone with God among hundreds of worshippers around me, the words God had stilled me with days earlier rested again on my heart: *Do not fear. I am allowing you to go through this for a reason.* I smiled slightly as calm washed over me once again.

> *For it is better, if it is God's will, to suffer for doing good*
> *than for doing evil. For Christ also suffered once for sins,*
> *the righteous for the unrighteous, to bring you to God.*
> *He was put to death in the body but made alive in the Spirit.*
> 1 Peter 3:17–18 NIV

When we're doing good, doing what God has asked of us, we don't typically envision suffering or being slandered because of it. We expect to be praised, affirmed, or held in high esteem, right?

But what if we're not? What if we suffer? What then?

The words of our pastor felt like they had been written with my ears in mind, and I listened intently to every word. "Have confidence God will bless you," he said. Referencing 1 Peter 3:14, he continued, "God's favor will be upon you as you live in a counter cultural setting. If when you do good, and yet suffer for it, you endure. This is a gracious thing in the sight of God."

> *"You're blessed when your commitment to*
> *God provokes persecution. The persecution drives you*
> *even deeper into God's kingdom.*
> *Not only that—count yourselves blessed every time people*
> *put you down or throw you out or speak lies*
> *about you to discredit me. What it means is that the truth*
> *is too close for comfort and they are uncomfortable.*
> *You can be glad when that happens—*
> *give a cheer, even!—for though they don't like it, I do!*
> *And all heaven applauds. And know that you*
> *are in good company. My prophets and witnesses*
> *have always gotten into this kind of trouble."*
> Matthew 5:10–12 MSG

The Lord told me, *Do not fear*, and both 1 Peter 3 and Matthew 5 reminded me once again that I need not do so. Peter certainly experienced suffering for his faith, and for doing good for the kingdom, he suffered much more than I likely ever will. Yet he had confidence because he had an eternal perspective, a bigger picture.

> *"Don't be bluffed into silence by the threats of bullies.*
> *There's nothing they can do to your soul, your core being.*
> *Save your fear for God, who holds your*
> *entire life—body and soul—in his hands."*
> Matthew 10:28 MSG

Like I had to do when this case was filed against me, Peter instructed his readers to be prepared to defend what they believed (1 Peter 3:15), and to do it with gentleness and respect. As our Hurting One told their side of the story and what they had become convinced had happened, I had a choice. I could have gotten upset and interrupted, telling the ladies from Child Protective Services that what our child was saying was completely untrue. I could have gotten fire in my eyes or burst into tears. But even before I sat in the sanctuary listening to this poignant sermon, I knew in my heart what was right.

Grace. Gentleness. Respect. These things were much more powerful. So when my child spoke with the women from Child Protective Services, I sat quietly, listening to my child as they relayed a story that, if believed, had the potential to completely change the lives of our entire family forever. Because Child Protective Services likely wouldn't be only taking this one child away, they'd potentially take all of them.

Exactly one week after these women from the state walked into our home, potentially loading not just our Hurting One but *all* our children into their cars and out of our lives, I sat on a hard chair at a round table in my Bible study, a hot latte in my hands. And the Spirit-led women who sat around me asked to pray for our family. The lifting of their sweet words to our loving Father warmed me to my core. Through their petitioning my pain to our Creator, I encountered a warmth that my coffee on that snowy morning could never emulate or compete with. What a blessing it was to open myself up, showing the dirt and pain in my life, letting others enter in to authentically see that my life was far from easy and eons away from perfect. By allowing them to join in and pray for me, they lifted up words to heaven that my heavy heart had a hard time mouthing. I believed every word they said, and yet I was too weary to whisper them myself.

If two or three of you come together as a community
and discern clearly about anything, My Father in heaven
will bless that discernment. For when two or three
gather together in My name, I am there in the midst of them.
Matthew 18:19–20 VOICE

An hour after leaving these women who so graciously went to the throne in prayer for me and my family, I received a call from Ben. As I cut lunch into bite-size pieces for now one-year-old Elsabet, my husband read the simple and yet weighty e-mail he had just received from Child Protective Services. "We have no concerns about the health and safety of your family," it read. "This case is closed."

I breathed again for the first time in days.

My mind couldn't decide whether to shriek in relief and excitement or to fall into the fetal position and sob. *Truth shone through*, I thought as I closed my eyes and quietly thanked God while picking up a piece of avocado Elsabet had just thrown.

The suggestion to "live in such a way that if anyone should speak badly of you no one would believe it," drifted through my mind. I am far from perfect and I fail daily, but these employees of the state whose job is solely to ensure the safety and well-being of children could see in me—in our family—the essence of that very statement. *Oh Lord, how I pray I continue to live in such a manner that light continues to shine upon Your truth.*

Our Hurting One saw how we as parents didn't give up on them. Our child, whose past is full of still-fresh wounds, wasn't made a fool again for placing their trust in someone. There really was a thing called unconditional love; it wasn't just something people said, or a hope, or a dream. It wasn't merely a word. This dark time needed to happen for our sweet child to see that. It was deeply important for them to see we were willing to stand by them, even in the venomous hurt and devastation they attempted to cause. *You really are doing a new thing, Father. I see it. I feel it.* Our child saw our love would not be squashed, and we were now on the other side. For a while anyway.

Taking Elsabet from her seat, I cuddled her while walking toward the kitchen sink to clean the now-smooshed avocado from her face, fingers, and hair—when I stopped. Blinking, I saw our hardwoods turn to lush green grass, leafy emerald foliage sprouting from the baseboards, winding itself up the walls and around the doorknobs. Flowers ablaze in brilliant hues of lemon yellow, saffron, fuchsia, and coral opened and seemed to smile at me in recognition of His glory. It was as if the Lord was telling me the clouds had parted, and as they did, the heavy and oppressive blackness that pulsed through our house like the Smoke Monster on *Lost* was chased away. Christ's light shone down onto our home and onto our family in the form of love and faithfulness.

God didn't give up on us when we needed Him most, just like we didn't give up on our child when abuse and neglect changed their view of what a family is.

I stood there silently, avocado slime from chubby one-year-old fingers being spread over my face, my arms, my shirt. Looking around, I smiled. But when I blinked again, real life returned. The scraped wooden floor once again showed muddy paw prints and misplaced Cheerios, the walls were soft gray, and the molding was bright white. My heavenly garden kitchen was gone. Carrying Elsabet the rest of the way to the sink, I acknowledged the vision in my mind's eye to be a gift from the Lord as He gave insight into the fruit He was promising to breathe into the walls of our once decrepit home. No longer was it uninhabitable physically, but it also breathed new life spiritually.

As joy poured in through the baseboards and keyholes, I understood God's promise that we needed to go through this pain for a reason. He was right, of course. I don't know why I was surprised in the slightest. We had gone to war and won. To God be the glory.

Since meeting with these ladies from CPS, I remember so clearly how I asked for prayer on so many sides. I was not, and am not, embarrassed about these accusations.

Through allowing myself to be vulnerable, which I like the idea of and yet it still makes me enormously uncomfortable to do, I live outstretched as an example of how God invites us to draw closer to Him through imperfect and messy lives and yet still blesses with joy.

Encircling each and every storm, I learn to lean into Him harder and closer. It's as if He's bending over, reaching down with hands stretched toward where I stand, waiting for me to take joy from His strong hands. This joy is yet another undeserved gift He's giving, and I need simply take and hold tightly. He tells me, *Take this joy. Take it. It's here to run your fingers over, to feel the realness of. It's My gift to you. Take it. Take joy.* And I have a choice to take this present—this too-good-to-be-true gift from my Father in heaven. He's already bought it for me. It's available and ready to be used; I need only to take hold of it and believe it's mine. Sometimes, though, I reach out but draw my hand back quickly before touching it because the Evil One's whispers are so loud I think this gift belongs to someone else and not to me.

But on this day I take it, realizing its depth and yet the way it feels light on my countenance, and I pray that He can use my experiences to support and comfort others as they go through their own darkness.

. . . 🦢 . . .

When CPS came and questioned our family, I was prepared to defend and fight for myself and my family. But in the day-to-day, are we prepared to defend Christ? I'm not talking about big, dramatic times like the one I was facing. I mean in our normal day, as we live in this cross-cultural world that is our home away from home. Are we ready to give an answer, a defense for the truth? And if so, can our hearts be so full of love that we do it with the gentleness and respect that Peter talked about? I pray that we are.

Your life as a Christian should make nonbelievers
question their disbelief in God.
Unknown

While reading 1 Corinthians 13 at the table that evening with my child, as I explained that if we are brash, disrespectful, or rude, we will turn people off, I felt those words pour into my own veins as well. Would you listen? Would I? No, likely not. Instead, we need to respect the person. Not only in theory, but in action. Respect their views, their backgrounds, their religious beliefs. Respect them as individuals, because if we don't, all they will hear is the sound of a clanging cymbal. Their mind and heart will turn away. And then, what's the point of saying anything at all? We could do more damage to God's work in them than if we had said nothing at all. Respect must be shown before truth can be given.

Only, live your life in a manner worthy of the gospel of Christ,
so that, whether I come and see you or am absent
and hear about you, I will know that you are standing firm
in one spirit, striving side by side
with one mind for the faith of the gospel.
Philippians 1:27 NRSV

Through the years, I've begun to learn what it means to endure well. Instead of praying that God would take away my pain and hardship, I'm understanding the importance of requesting that He strengthen me enough to walk through it. I could either be destroyed by this or I could fall to my knees, with tear-filled eyes turned toward heaven, and pray the words of Jill Briscoe: "Toughen me up, God."[18] We need to learn to pray for a holy toughness, so I'm stopping to pray for us now: *Lord, help not only me but the heart attached to the set of eyes that pour over these pages. I ask that we learn how to endure and persevere. Teach us, Father. Do a new thing in response to this moment and any moment we experience that deeply hurts to walk through.*

CHAPTER 15

. . . .

Firstfruits

. . . . 🦢 . . . .

You were not created to live
small and safe,
you were created to live
fierce and brave.
—LISA BEVERE

Life doesn't need to be full of darkness for our souls to become weary and exhausted. Sometimes it's as if I need to give myself permission to remember how even good things that fill my schedule and my day can drain me as my buckets pour out.

Here I sit on the couch, laptop propped up against me, as I try, ever so hard, to ignore the pounding of the men putting on our new roof after a storm with golf ball sized hail put holes in our home large enough to make it rain inside. This roof was supposed to have been done months ago, but whatever. At least it'll be completed before the Denver snow begins and poor weather conditions force us to wait till next spring.

I am worn out today. Weary. Exhausted. Ben has been out of town a lot lately and the kids haven't napped in days because of all the roof clatter. I'm not too shy to admit it: I need a break.

I prayed (and prayed and prayed) that the kids could somehow sleep today. That the Lord would close their ears to all this banging, hammering, and walking around above their heads. Because I am about to lose my mind.

And you know what? Though I keep checking on them, they're out. Completely out. *(Thank You, Jesus.)*

Have you ever heard the song "Worn" by Tenth Avenue North? I play it over and over these days. It fills my soul with so much hope and promise that even though I'm beat down and exhausted, I'll make it through as I continue to seek God's face.

With lyrics like "I'm worn, even before the day begins" and "I want to know a song can rise from the ashes of a broken life," it fits so well with what I'm feeling and seeing as we continue to settle in as a family and heal broken hearts.[19]

Sometimes I feel like I don't know what I'm doing. Well, to be honest, much of the time I truly don't. But that's when I'm reminded of this:

> *"Remain in me, as I also remain in you.*
> *No branch can bear fruit by itself; it must remain in the vine.*
> *Neither can you bear fruit unless you remain in me.*
> *I am the vine; you are the branches.*
> *If you remain in me and I in you, you will bear much fruit;*
> *apart from me you can do nothing."*
> John 15:4–5 NIV

I need to learn to *remain* in Him. In other words, if I become disconnected from the Vine (God is the Vine; John 15:5), there's no way I'll be successful and bear fruit. I won't make it, as a good mom, a loving wife, or simply plain ol' me.

But how do I do that? How do I learn to remain in Him? Simply put, I need to follow Him, rather than leading myself and controlling everything.

I can't see all . . .

know all . . .

do all . . .

But He can.

And He does.

Peace, love, compassion, and joy become as juicy and tangible as a perfectly ripened apple or pear when we follow the Lord and His precepts. As we live a life more like Jesus, He'll not only lead us but will also give this spiritual fruit as gifts that will be seen as evidence that we live in relationship with Him.

Supernatural strength is another gift from above, and one I'm desperately needing lately. Strength to keep going, to keep smiling. Strength to keep from running to the beaches of Mexico and never coming back.

In my quiet time this morning, Isaiah 43 is where I turned. And though my study wasn't talking about weariness, but rather my true identity as a daughter of Christ, it struck my heart heavily as I read His promise to us.

"When you pass through the waters, I will be with you;
and when you pass through the rivers,
they will not sweep over you.
When you walk through the fire,
you will not be burned;
the flames will not set you ablaze."
Isaiah 43:2 NIV

I know He will be with me right where I am. Deep down, I know that I know it. *But* it doesn't necessarily mean I always feel or remember it. Yet it's written right there in black and white in the Bible I hold in my hands. So why can't I think those same thoughts for my own life? I wanted Him to use me, right? Well . . . He is. He's wearing me out and wearing me in, like my favorite pair of jeans from Anthropologie.

God promises to be with me. He promises that the waters will not sweep over me, and even if I'm walking through the fire, I will not be burned. Maybe I'll even be refined (Zechariah 13:9; Isaiah 48:10), but nowhere does it say life will be easy and nowhere does the Bible share that those making the biggest impact for the kingdom were the ones sipping lemonade while relaxing near the Nile.

I'm slowly discovering through my exhaustion that He is breaking me with a sort of Sacred Brokenness—that my messy and chipped life has been torn and messed up for a divine purpose. It seems to me that this isn't a bad thing or something to be fearful of, but rather a blessing. Didn't I ask Him to send me, to use me, all those years ago? I didn't specify that He only use me when I felt like it. Or when I've had enough sleep.

When I close my eyes, I imagine myself kneeling before the Lord as He sits upon His throne. My head is bowed, hiding the tears and bags under my eyes. My arms are loaded full of my weakness, weariness, imperfection, and my desire to control everything from my children's behavior to keeping up a perfectly clean house, but I raise it all up to Him as if to say:

> *Here, God, take it. I can't handle it. It's too much. Lord, You have said, "I will refresh the weary and satisfy the faint" (Jeremiah 31:25 NIV). Help me open my heart to receive that, Jesus.*
>
> *Help me remain in You. Help me remember that apart from You, I can do nothing. You say that if I remain in Your love, Your joy will reside within me (John 15:9–12 NIV). I need that, Lord. Fill me with Your love. Help me show my family Your light and Your love. Draw me closer to Your side, Father.*

I'm so thankful that nothing is a surprise to Him. He already knew that I couldn't do this all on my own. I can't and you can't.

> *Don't run from tests and hardships, brothers and sisters. As difficult as they are, you will ultimately find joy in them; if you embrace them, your faith will blossom under pressure and teach you true patience as you endure. And true patience brought on by endurance will equip you to complete the long journey and cross the finish line—mature, complete, and wanting nothing.*
>
> James 1:2 VOICE

I encourage you to find joy through the struggles, through the weariness. I've said it before and I'll say it again: *take joy.* Grab it with both hands and don't let go, for the Lord has promised us great things if we come to Him (and yes, I am looking in the mirror as I say this).

"Come to me, all you who are weary and burdened,
and I will give you rest. Take my yoke upon you and learn from me,
for I am gentle and humble in heart, and you will find rest
for your souls. For my yoke is easy and my burden is light."
Matthew 11:28–30 NIV

... 🦢 ...

Days sped by, years actually, and suddenly we were out of the home with a new roof, the one that was deemed uninhabitable, that is now dreamy, updated, and safe. We find ourselves now in yet another house, one I'm still calling our current home.

Elsabet is no longer an infant, and as much as I'd love for them to, our kids rarely take naps. Instead, as I now sit at the desk in the kitchen, attempting to work, I watch through the window as our darling girls play in the backyard. In a gentle, rhythm-like cadence—almost hypnotizing—their dark little knees pump as they go higher and higher on their beloved swings. Abandoned only a moment later, the swings hang discarded, still swaying back and forth, awaiting another ride.

Onto the slide the girls climb, giggling sweetly together, as they often do . . . and then the little one smacks the older upside the head and the candy-coated moment is gone. Instantly replaced with fighting, crying, and screaming.

I sigh and roll my eyes, saving what I'd just typed on the mostly blank computer screen. Trying not to be annoyed as I wish I hadn't been disrupted. *Again.* And knowing my train of thought will dissolve in the morning sun as soon as I open the screen door to both soothe and reprimand my little Ethiopian loves.

With our large family, rarely is there a quiet and serene moment. Rarely can I complete a task in one sitting. Sometimes I don't complete it at all. Long is my list of to-dos: meals to make and laundry to fold, blog posts and book chapters to write.

The question that constantly parades through my thoughts is: *How on earth can I do it all?* Well, simply put—I can't. And neither can you.

It doesn't matter if you have six kids or one. Maybe you don't have kids, but your commitments pull at you from all directions.

Here's my advice to you: give up.

I know what you're thinking: *Give up?!* Just bear with me another minute.

My mom always says, "*Major in the majors and minor in the minors.*" Have you heard that before? The concept is simple: take the time for what's important, the major things. Spend time on those things; do those well.

The minor matters and concerns constantly surround, and yet life doesn't fall apart if they're not done. Sort of like my heavily underlined, dog-eared copies of Lysa TerKeurst's book *The Best Yes* and Shauna Niequist's *Present over Perfect*. They're fantastic books, but we don't need to read every page to understand what they're getting at: Step back. Prioritize. Spend your *yesses* wisely.

I can't begin to tell you how many things I've said no to this week alone.

Good things, even godly things, can become idols or distractions when we don't set boundaries and distinctions.

Our kids? We don't get do-overs with them. We don't get to push on their heads and shrink them down tiny again. This is it. God first, husband second, kids third. We all know that, but what does it really mean?

We need to make time with God. Quiet, just-the-two-of-us time. It doesn't matter when in the day it's done, as long as it's not when you're falling asleep or distracted and unengaged in your moments *with* Him. Before our kids all slept through the night, I did my devotions during naptime, but now I get up before the rest of the family. That's what works for me.

We try to tuck in the kids between 7:30 and 8:00 p.m. every evening so Ben and I can spend time together before we, too, close our eyes for the night. Our older boys stay up later studying, but if they've done all they need to do, they know to head to bed and read or journal until their official lights-out. It's so very important for Ben and me to spend time together in the evenings, just the two of us catching up on the day as we clean the kitchen together or fold a pile of laundry. And then after perhaps relaxing outside on the porch. Or watching a show as we cuddle up on the couch. Or reading books in bed with our feet entwined. Something simple.

Love isn't the colossal moments. It's the small ones piled up that make it so monumental.

Similar to the importance of spending quality time with our spouse, it is imperative with our children. Saying yes to the Slip 'n Slide in the rain before bed (which we did the other night). Having a picnic dinner in the backyard. Piling books and water bottles and blankets into a wagon and finding the perfect spot at the park to read. Just saying yes a little more to the simple things.

No, we cannot do it all. We might as well give up that fantasy now. But we *can* do the little things, one by one, because piled upon one another, they won't be seen as minor or as insignificant. Little moments won't remain infinitesimal but will be celebrated instead as big memories that last a lifetime. No matter how busy we are, we make memories every day. What types of memories are you capturing?

Express to the Lord your own version of the Prayer of Jabez. Though just a quick blip within the pages of Scripture, the life of this man is one of great remembrance because of how his heart was positioned to the Lord.

> *Jabez called on the God of Israel, saying,*
> *"Oh that you would bless me and enlarge my border,*

*and that your hand might be with me, and that you would
keep me from hurt and harm!" And God granted what he asked.*
1 Chronicles 4:10 NRSV

Give your plans back over to Christ and allow Him to form a new thing within your life. Allow yourself to be beautifully interrupted. God will lead you to something with an incredible passion and calling. But when that calling or your purpose is fulfilled, don't think for a second that you're done! The exciting thing is discovering how He will use your experiences to bring you to yet another place you're needed.

It's cyclical, really. Around and around we go as the Lord sets us into motion, being put into action for God's kingdom.

I can say this now and urge you of its importance because the Lord has brought us though the fire. I haven't always "gotten it" and have sunk deeper and deeper into a pit of exhaustion and ineffectiveness. Sometimes we have to capsize and disappear beneath the waves. Sometimes we have to hit the bottom, or at least near the lowermost chasm of the abyss, so we remember how much we need Him and cling white-knuckled to the Lord as He ultimately pulls us out.

There are moments and seasons that hurt something fierce but are also so freeing with the knowledge that going through them is a necessity for our future strength and relationship with God. One such season occurred just after we brought Ezekiel home and Ben's job began to change.

We were still so new to this whole adoption thing and were suddenly thrown into more transitions as Ben began traveling back and forth from San Antonio to Portland every month. He'd be gone five days of the month and spend more time in the office, which I look back on as the most exhausting and overwhelming time of my life caring for and loving a four-year-old, a three-year-old, an infant, and our newest addition, a six-year-old who spoke almost no English and whom we were having challenges with as his heart began to heal.

I remember collapsing onto the floor in the kitchen one afternoon and bursting into tears. As I sat there on the cold tile floor holding baby Imani, Anton and Laith both crawled onto my lap, cuddling and comforting me, while Ezekiel stared with wide eyes a few feet away. I wondered how on earth I could do this. I have so much respect for single parents and military families. I could barely endure a week per month by myself.

> Give your plans back over to Christ and allow Him to form a new thing within your life. Allow yourself to be beautifully interrupted.

Lord, is this really what we're supposed to be doing? You've got to give me more strength for this! I absolutely cannot do it on my own. That day was a turning point for me. I certainly wasn't at rock bottom, but I was drowning. I needed to cling to Him tighter. I had to, or I wasn't going to survive.

> *But those who trust in the LORD will find new strength.*
> *They will soar high on wings like eagles.*
> *They will run and not grow weary.*
> *They will walk and not faint.*
> Isaiah 40:31 NLT

Though the very essence of my soul wailed at the notion of being so low that my tiny children were compelled to crawl on the ground to comfort *me*, the reality was that I desperately needed their unyielding love while sobbing on that floor. And at that moment, God also bestowed their sweet tenderness to remind me of Himself. That His love is also unyielding and tender.

As I ugly cried on the floor, being cared for by my precious preschool-age children, God whispered the word *firstfruits* into my ear.

Pausing from my tears for a moment, my mind began working like a Rolodex, trying to comprehend how it applied to me and my season. *Firstfruits?* I asked, confused. *Help me understand what You mean, Lord!*

I knew that firstfruits are offerings of the first and best crops to God, which is often spoken about in the Old Testament. It was an offering given in acknowledgment of God's abundant blessing. Definitely not giving Him what is left over, but rather giving Him the best of the best *first*.

> *And there is more; it's not just creation—all of us*
> *are groaning together too. Though we have already tasted*
> *the firstfruits of the Spirit, we are longing for the total*
> *redemption of our bodies that comes when our adoption*
> *as children of God is complete.*
> Romans 8:23 VOICE

What was I giving Him? The leftovers. The leftovers of my time, my energy, and my heart. He was reminding me of the need to put Him first. Above everything. Though I was going to Bible study every week, I wasn't really spending time with Him. My quiet time, my devotions, my reading of the Bible and prayer time—it was sporadic and hurried. My heart was for Him, but I was in survival mode and He'd somehow gotten left behind in all the craziness and exhaustion that had become my life.

I was being tossed like a ship in a storm. I felt alone and overwhelmed. I was exhausted by the new challenges we faced as a family. I knew nothing could separate me from the Lord, that He was stronger and more powerful than this storm, but I was lost in the wind and waves. What I realized that day was that I needed to have the right perspective of Him. I needed to lean into the Lord and live in a posture of humility. My eyes were opened to the necessity of being bold in prayer, regardless of how I felt. I needed—no, I *had* to take the time for Him or there would be nothing of me left. I was encouraged with immediate relief knowing that giving Him my firstfruits would not only keep me off the floor but would also help me become an unconquerable force because I would be living in His power.

I wasn't sleeping much at night since Imani wasn't, Ben was gone for what felt like a lot of the time, and I simply couldn't get ahead of anything. The house never seemed clean; the laundry never ended; the sink was never empty of dishes. I didn't know how to ask for help. I had family and many friends who would have dropped everything to help me if they'd known how much I was struggling, yet I felt I had to put on a brave, smiling face all the time.

I felt (and still struggle with feeling this way) that I had no business asking for help from anyone. This was the life Ben and I chose. We *chose* to have this many children. We *chose* to have a family that is outside the norm, full of things we're still learning how to handle and love through.

Things like how to teach a child English. How to help a young boy heal his hurt and loss and understand that we love him no matter how hard he tries to push us away. How to help two towheaded preschool-age boys not to feel ignored, or replaced, or that our adopted kids are more important to us than they are, even though they're requiring a lot of extra attention.

Take some of the firstfruits of all that you produce
from the soil of the land the Lord your God is giving you
and put them in a basket. Then go to the place
the Lord your God will choose as a dwelling for his Name.
Deuteronomy 26:2 NIV

Firstfruits.
Well, I didn't have a lamb or crops to give, but I certainly had my firstfruits of time. I was so sleep-deprived and exhausted from Imani

waking multiple times a night that there was no way—*no way*—I could get up earlier. I knew mornings were out.

I felt the Lord direct me, saying to give my firstfruits during naptime. Rather than scurrying through the house cleaning up, doing laundry, and tackling the constant stream of dishes, I was called to *first* sit and be with Him. Then do my tasks *after*.

And it changed everything.

I don't mean to say that everything became sunny all the time, but it was suddenly manageable. My attitude was better, and I had a full grasp on things.

Jesus loved me back to life. My season changed.

Somehow I was receiving a divine amount of ability and productivity. The Lord was multiplying my time, renewing and energizing me. I could see His hand in my life as my patience grew. Grace was extended toward our family and kindness was electrified. Magnified. I was more attentive and loving, and my tasks were not only being completed but being executed thoroughly, and well. And through it all, I confidently leaned on Him, knowing it was in His power, not my own, that it was all getting done.

Two years later, I felt God stretching me once again. Encouraging me toward waking up earlier and spending an hour or two with Him before our children begin to stir in the morning, He released me of my precious naptime in the middle of the day.

> *In the morning, Lord, you hear my voice;*
> *in the morning I lay my requests before you*
> *and wait expectantly.*
> Psalm 5:3 NIV

Whenever I talk about how early I rise, people seem rather shocked that I wake several hours before my children. Assuming I'm some sort of crazy morning person, they often announce to me, "Oh I could *neeeever* do that. I'm just too tired. I need my sleep."

Oh, if you only knew, I want to tell them!

I so struggle getting up in the morning. Ben says I'm just like the kids: exhausted in the evening yet forced to actually crawl into bed. I want to stay up! I've always been more of a night person. So when my alarm chimes, I just want to cozy even deeper into my blankets and enjoy the warmth of my bed.

Get up! Get up! I urge myself.

Grab your Bible and make a coffee . . . go! I tell myself as I convince my sleepy body to push back the covers.

Every morning I ask myself, *What's more important, my relationship with Christ or with my pillow?*

My day is genuinely so much better once I've started it in the Word and in prayer. My attitude is better and I'm more focused, more joyful, less likely to snap at my kids and husband. My family even notices it.

> *Honor the* LORD *with your wealth,*
> *with the firstfruits of all your crops;*
> *then your barns will be filled to overflowing,*
> *and your vats will brim over with new wine.*
> Proverbs 3:9–10 NIV

My mind often races, full of the things I need to do, groceries I need to buy, and schedules I need to manage. So I've learned to have a journal next to me. Once I quickly scribble down whatever is rattling through my brain, keeping me from truly being able to concentrate, I can move on and move closer in my time with my Lord.

> *I urge you to live a life worthy of the calling you have received.*
> *Be completely humble and gentle;*
> *be patient, bearing with one another in love.*
> Ephesians 4:1–2 NIV

As my time magnified, the way I saw things also changed. I began to realize what an *honor* it was to care for my family. Keeping the house picked up didn't make me a glorified maid; it was my *privilege* to take care of them in this way. I'm not going to lie and tell you that I suddenly turned into Mother Teresa or walked around with a halo over my head, never complaining when the kids spilled their milk for the fourth time that day.

I still prayed daily that God would work in me to give me a good attitude, patience, and strength so that I wouldn't lose my temper with my family because things weren't as perfect as I wanted them to be. But as my time of intimacy increased, my whole being began to blossom with fruit. The storm that I felt was going to drown me instead made me stronger because it led me back to Him.

My suffering was good for me, for it taught me
to pay attention to your decrees.
Your instructions are more valuable to me
than millions in gold and silver.
You made me; you created me.
Now give me the sense to follow your commands.
May all who fear you find in me a cause for joy,
for I have put my hope in your word.
Psalm 119:71–74 NLT

CHAPTER 16

· · · · · · · · · · · · · ·

Now Live Like It

· · · · · · · 🦢 · · · · · · · ·

*There is no passion to be found playing small—
in settling for a life that is less than
the one you are capable of living.*

NELSON MANDELA

Life got intense for the disciples when they followed Christ. These men were mocked, ridiculed, and stretched beyond anything they thought they could withstand. When some of His followers began to leave because it was getting too difficult—too costly—Jesus looked at His twelve and inquired, "Will you leave Me too?" (paraphrase of John 6:67).

I want to be counted with those twelve. I want to stay. I can't give up, I won't. Life isn't easy. Sometimes it's more difficult than I have energy for, but He put a desire into my heart so many years ago that my borders would be expanded. I opened my heart and gave Him permission to stretch me and deepen my impact.

I want Him more now than ever.

I have a deep desire to make a difference. My world shouldn't involve only me. What a small world that would be if it were indeed how we were supposed to live.

I want my world to outlive me, for it to be very little about what I've done but rather how I've loved.

Our Lord continues to heal the broken hearts of our children who have painful pasts. But we must allow Him to bind our own wounds and heal us too. He knows us. He understands our struggles, and He *will* bless us as each of us seeks Him and puts our false self to rest.

I've done a horrible job with baby books, so I love when Facebook reminds me what was posted on that day, years prior. One of my favorite reminders ever was originally written on Abreham's first day of school in the US:

Last night I went in to say good night and pray with Abreham and Ezekiel. Abreham looked at me with a big smile and said, "Daddy, tomorrow school." I asked him if he was scared. He put his hand on his heart and patted it to show the feeling of his heart beating rapidly from being scared. "Yeah, scared."

It struck me powerfully at that moment and again this morning how brave this boy is. Too often with older adoptive children people think that they are coming to America so things will be better. What is forgotten is that everything about their culture is ripped from them as they fly from Ethiopia to America. They may not have the luxuries we have but they have the ability to understand and communicate with people. They know the food, the smells, and cultural norms. They know where they fit and what to expect. They just know things . . . good or bad.

When they get to America there is no way they could possibly accurately understand what's coming. If you have ever been to a third-world country, close your eyes and go back there. Now try to possibly think of America if all you know is that country. No way.

The smells are new, the houses huge, the schools huge, the language, the food . . . nothing is the same. Nothing is known. There is no safe, comforting place that you know you belong. You don't even know your family that well.

Abreham fought to get a chance to continue his education and to see him acknowledge that he was really scared was touching. The bravery is that there was no hesitation. He was scared but that didn't matter. He was going to walk into a school with hundreds (maybe thousands) of kids he could not speak to and sit in a classroom without knowing anyone.

I dropped him off this morning and watched him look back with a nervous smile, then he turned and walked into school. I felt like a mom dropping her little kid off at kindergarten or

first grade. It was emotional. I was scared for him but so unbe-
lievably proud of him.

He will struggle, succeed, and fail many times during this
journey, but even in the little time we have known him there is
no question that he will fight through it.

He is brave enough to be scared and still face forward into
the unknown. We are so proud of you, Abreham.

Ben's Facebook post from August 19, 2013

It's fascinating how each and every time we go through a rough season (sometimes really rough), we end up stronger in the end. Ben
and I lean harder on each other and on Christ. The kids form an
impenetrable bond, to one another and to Ben and me.

It's like we've been to battle and won, bringing the spoils of war
into our family. In our case, the spoils being an abundant understanding of uncompromising love, unwavering dedication, and the
fortitude to both stand firm and press on.

We refuse to let Satan win.

Some friends have asked if I want to just give up at times.

No. Not even kind of.

"You're familiar with the old written law, 'Love your friend,'
and its unwritten companion, 'Hate your enemy.' I'm challeng-
ing that. I'm telling you to love your enemies. Let them bring out
the best in you, not the worst. When someone gives you a hard
time, respond with the energies of prayer, for then you are work-
ing out of your true selves, your God-created selves. This is what
God does. He gives his best—the sun to warm and the rain to
nourish—to everyone, regardless: the good and bad, the nice
and nasty. If all you do is love the lovable, do you expect a bonus?

*Anybody can do that. If you simply say hello to those who greet
you, do you expect a medal? Any run-of-the-mill sinner does that.*

*In a word, what I'm saying is, Grow up. You're kingdom
subjects. Now live like it. Live out your God-created identity.
Live generously and graciously toward others, the way God lives
toward you."*

Matthew 5:43–48 MSG

When I read books, as well as passages from the Bible, it's typically a conversation not only between me and God but often a conversation back to myself. I suppose that's why the margins of my Bible and all my books are chock-full of my own commentary, big scripted question marks, and multiple exclamations of "Yes!".

"When someone gives you a hard time, respond with the energies of prayer." (Yes!)

"If all you do is love the lovable, do you expect a bonus? Anybody can do that. If you simply say hello to those who greet you, do you expect a medal? Any run-of-the-mill sinner does that." (Ugh. Okay, I'm listening.)

"In a word, what I'm saying is, Grow up. You're kingdom subjects. Now live like it." (Grow up and live like it. Oh, how I want to.)

Perhaps it's just me that reads interactively like this, but here and now, I'm wrapping my calloused and weary fingers around this promise:

*Now to him who is able to do immeasurably more than all we
ask or imagine, according to his power that is at work within us,
to him be glory in the church and in Christ Jesus throughout all
generations, for ever and ever! Amen.*

Ephesians 3:20–21 NIV

That's big. And it's scary.

Remember, we're not perfect. We *will* stumble. And falling is inevitable. But when we're walking closely with Christ, we have an opportunity to let it strengthen rather than define us. Let those times of missteps be fewer and further between as we learn from each of these moments and experiences. Once we know better, do better. Be better.

The painful and dramatic episodes from the hurt of our children's past have begun to lessen in intensity and frequency. They are learning each time they come unglued. They continue growing in our love and consistency. Learning their own triggers. Figuring out what works to help them heal.

The love of Christ continues to help them, and us, become well and whole.

> *He heals the brokenhearted*
> *and binds up their wounds.*
> *He determines the number of the stars*
> *and calls them each by name.*
> Psalm 147:3–4 NIV

A few years ago, Ben traveled to Washington, DC, for the Marine Corps Marathon. Up late one of the evenings he was gone, I was enjoying time by myself and control of the remote—until a *bang bang bang* on the front door turned my sweetly predicable Hallmark movie into what felt like a Lifetime special. Freezing, I shrunk down low into the couch, hoping and praying doing so meant the crazy person at my door couldn't see me through the windows on either side of the entry into our home. *Why, oh why, did I insist on those windows when we got our new door? It's terrifyingly simple to see me through that glass,* I thought to myself with eyes wide and full of fear.

I felt silly sitting there, my rational mind telling me it was probably one of our older boy's friends. I thought of all the times my brother and I played tricks on our friends as teenagers. Hearing no other noise, I eventually let go of the breath I had apparently been holding, scooched my body upright, and went back to watching my movie. Ten or so minutes later, the fist on our front door pounded again.

I have what you could call a simmering and animated imagination. You know, a healthy (sometimes not so healthy) fear of what "could be." Maybe it was our experiences in Guatemala, or police stories from my dad, or too many action movies. But I'm not going to lie, I kind of freaked. Calling Ben from my cell phone, I whispered frantically as I crouched into the deep recesses of the couch, making myself as small and unseen as possible. "Babe, what I should do?" My voice quivered in fear a little as I spoke.

Not feeling the terror that I did—nor having the overactive imagination—and being on the other side of the country, Ben had the ridiculous notion of simply opening the door to see who was out there. "Are you crazy?" I countered. "And be chopped up or something?" I hung up on him, muttering harshly, "Forget it! You can't help me!"

Stuffing my phone into my back pocket, I scrambled upstairs and woke Abreham. I told him my story as he sat up rubbing his eyes. "It's okay, Mommy, I come downstairs." Grabbing Ezekiel's lacrosse stick, we headed to the front door to investigate. He raised the stick up high over his shoulder like it was a baseball bat and was about to hit a winning home run, and whispered for me to open the door quickly while he'd swing.

As the door swung open, he stopped and lowered his so-called weapon. We looked down to the mat at the front door and there lay a pumpkin full of candy and a note that said, "You've been booed."

Exhale.

We laughed and rolled our eyes for getting so worked up and

sat down at the kitchen table, riffling through the candy looking for chocolate, while I explained to him that being "booed" meant an anonymous friend or neighbor would leave a bucket of treats at your door with the instructions of doing it to someone else. Typically, though, I said, it's not done so late in the night.

Motioning to the lacrosse stick, I teased him and thanked my then-fourteen-year-old for protecting me. He cracked a smile, his eyes wrinkling as the silver of his braces shone brightly.

We sat there at the same crumb-covered table where we had sat so many times before during some of our hard seasons. But on this night, we settled into our seats munching on Halloween candy while my newest son announced that he'd always protect me, that I'm his mommy and he loves me. I continue to swoon when my teenage son calls me Mommy. The disparity of our different seasons and conversations at that table did not escape me.

I leaned forward, looking deeply into his deep-brown eyes, and told him, "No, my sweet. It is Daddy's and my job to protect you." He knew I was talking about so much more than simply my overreacting to friends playing a trick on us. Abreham had chosen to keep his given name, but when a child is adopted from Ethiopia their middle and last names become that of the adoptive father. Abreham liked that his name had become Abreham Ben Anderson and that he had a connection to his new dad in this way. There was a deep bond forming between our hearts and his. A bond of protection and trust. A bond that says we're in this together and he never needs to be alone again. Because this is it. We are it. We're consistent and persistent. Our love is true, and it is not conditional. Hard days remain ahead for all of us, and yet by God's grace still we *remain*. We learn to do so because Jesus has remained with Ben and me through the years. I remind not only myself of this truth, but try to remind our kids during one of their hard seasons: God remains with us all, all the time.

He holds us in His very hands and cares deeply about all we encounter through every day and in every season we find ourselves in.

> *"Be strong and courageous. Do not be afraid or terrified*
> *because of them, for the LORD your God goes with you;*
> *he will never leave you nor forsake you."*
> Deuteronomy 31:6 NIV

This Old Testament passage may be talking about a conversation between Moses and Joshua as the incredible old man handed the leadership reins to his successor before his own death, and yet it's a reminder for us as well. Just to make sure we get it, it's said again a few verses later:

> *"Be strong and courageous . . . The LORD himself goes before you*
> *and will be with you; he will never leave you nor forsake you.*
> *Do not be afraid; do not be discouraged."*
> Deuteronomy 31:7–8 NIV

Be strong and don't give up. Be courageous and audacious. The Lord is walking through it all with us. Always.

Our children all have different stories, Ben and I do, too. We're all in need of different things, and even while living in the same house among the same loving family, we go through differing seasons: one of us may be feeling particularly wounded at the same moment another may cheerfully stand on a mountaintop. We've learned through the years that one emotion often flows into another, peace can quickly turn to worry, and uncertainty can flow back to confidence and hope. Because we all have such different stories, the kids know we have separate expectations for each of them. If they ever ask why one can do something the other cannot, we state simply, "because God used different cookie cutters for each of you. You're not the same exact cookie."

I say the same to you: your sister may struggle differently than you ever have, your best friend may not totally understand why a certain aspect of life trips you up the way it does. God created us as unique individuals and desired us to live in community with one another so that we can learn from each other and support one another. We cannot compare our suffering with someone else's suffering because all we know is what we're living. Similarly, we are not called to inspect others' fruit or to produce others' fruit. Our stories are unique and even the hard valleys have purpose.

For example, Abreham worked at a car wash last summer. It wasn't particularly close to our house and he had yet to get his driver's license so he took the light-rail each day. While walking under the overpass that led to where he'd buy his ticket and hop on the train, he'd often see a homeless man. Day after day, he'd smile and say hello as he passed the man. One morning though, Abreham was struck with the realization that this man had a story, and, just like the rest of us, he needed hope and community. Stopping to have a conversation with him, my teenage son wanted to know the narrative that was this man's life. According to the man, he struggled with family issues and since he was relatively new to our country, he didn't have a community or anyone to go to. This man came into our country legally, but no one wanted to hire a dirty homeless man who didn't speak English well. The Lord spoke to my son's heart that day and urged him to buy the hungry man breakfast at the nearby McDonald's as well as a ticket for the light-rail. Why the train ticket? Because Abreham was determined to get him a job at the car wash. And you know what? He did. And it wasn't the only

> He holds us in His very hands and cares deeply about all we encounter through every day and in every season we find ourselves in.

time our oldest son did something like this. Abreham didn't work at that car wash for more than a few months, yet when he'd hear of someone who couldn't find a job, he'd tell them to come by and tell his boss that he was the one who sent them. He did the same thing for a friend's sixty-five-year-old mother who came over from Ethiopia and also hardly spoke any English. He knew fluency wasn't a prerequisite to wash a car. He dove into these people's stories, knowing each was different, and because he listened to the Lord's prompting, he helped change the narrative in their lives.

How often do we do something like this? I'll admit . . . I never have to the extent Abreham has. Maybe it's a different type of bravery that I haven't tapped into yet, but watching my son sure has made me pay closer attention to how I can also enter into the stories of people I encounter each and every day. I remember awhile back someone telling me she struggled with all the devastation we hear about every day in the news: human trafficking, the global water crisis, children dying from hunger, domestic violence, and so many more horrible things. As she shared this struggle, she asked, "Where is God in all of this?" The other woman with us looked at her and gently said, "What if that's why we're here? What are *you* doing about it?" Gosh her comment woke me up: *What am I doing about it?* I can't complain and yet do nothing.

Sometimes God walks us through the valley, or through seasons in general, to show us something. Perhaps Abreham's short time at that car wash was just to help this man. Maybe my friend was struggling with all that she saw on the news because the Lord wanted her to wake up and take action. Our pastor recently did a series called "The Way of the Valley" and he pointed out that sometimes God takes us through this so-called lowland to show us the reality of something.[20] The place of frustration, anxiety, brokenness, or hopelessness can be a place of restoration and growth if we're willing to walk through it *with* Him, rather than blaming Him for the pain of it.

I can hear the Lord whisper into my heart, *I will take you through and into the beauty.*

I'm clinging to that promise as I type this while our family goes through something harder than we've gone through in a very long time. It's a devastating loss that really makes no sense. Right at this very moment, our hearts are broken and yet through the ache, I know there is purpose for each of us—as hard as it is for me to believe it now.

What will you learn from this? How will this help you trust Me more? I hear Him whisper.

God has rescued us before . . . do I trust Him enough to do it again? When King David was hiding in the wilderness first from Saul, and then again decades later as his own son wanted to kill him, he knew that God was near. He knew God loved him in a profound way and expected the Lord to move. In Psalm 63 (ESV), David tells God what he "will" do seven separate times. "My lips will praise you," ". . . in the shadow of your wings I will sing for joy." and so on. David had decided that even through hard times, he *will* keep moving. He *will* keep worshipping God through devastation. He *will* live bravely, courageously, and with expectation. David basically said, "Because I have seen You move before in the past, I know You will move in the future." David trusts this season will come to an end and the Lord will be with him before, during, and after it does, and His purpose will prevail. I believe the same for what our family is experiencing today.

> *He lifted me out of the slimy pit,*
> *out of the mud and mire; he set my feet on a rock*
> *and gave me a firm place to stand.*
> Psalm 40:2 NIV

There was a point in my life, many years ago, that God lifted me out of the muck and out of a really hard situation. Previously always holding my ground when it came to guys, I slid down into a hole I never thought I'd fall into. It was a brief time in the grand scheme of my life, but it shook me to my very core. I let a crack form in my relationship with Jesus and Satan jumped right up and wriggled his way through that crack, making it bigger and bigger until bad decisions were made and things couldn't be undone.

But God has most certainly used my mistakes for good, helping me now see how He orchestrated things through it. And I've gotten off that pedestal I didn't realize I'd placed myself on. I didn't think of myself as judgmental, but I see now that's exactly what I was. To anyone I hurt along the way, I'm sorry.

Had Christ not allowed me to tumble off that silly self-made pedestal, I genuinely don't think I would have married Ben. And now that you've read more about his story and our story together you'll see how God orchestrated my friendship with Ben with such perfect timing, shortly after falling off the pedestal and realizing I saw people through such judgmental lenses. I'm so glad the Lord brought him into my life when He did because I would have previously thought Ben's light wasn't shimmering enough for me. He had a hard time growing up and because of long-ago made decisions, I would have snubbed any possibility of a future with him. I'm so thankful Christ doesn't look at us through my same glasses and that He is a God of grace, forgiveness, and reconciliation.

> *Come, let's talk this over, says the LORD;*
> *no matter how deep the stain of your sins,*
> *I can take it out and make you as clean*
> *as freshly fallen snow. Even if you are stained*
> *as red as crimson, I can make you white as wool!*
> Isaiah 1:18 TLB

People are capable of absolutely anything. Provide a chink in the armor and the Evil One really will slither right on in.

On that incredible trip to Europe my parents took us on just after high school, we ended our time in England, where my dad spoke volumes about a Bible school up north called Capernwray, that he had wanted to attend when he was younger. Though he wanted to show it to Erik and me, we never made it outside London because we fell so head over heels for the allure of the city that spouts such magnificent museums and rich history.

Years passed and the idea of that school took root, growing to a desire so big that I had the application on the desk in my college dorm for a year. Finally tired of hearing me talk about it constantly, yet seeing the application collect dust because I was too scared to make the jump, my roommate, Lissy, filled it out for me. I was breathless when I got in, hugging her and jumping up and down. Six months later, Erik and I traveled together on a quick trip to Scotland before he dropped me at a school reminiscent of the grounds on *Downton Abbey*. Surrounded by nothing but rolling hills and sheep, yet regal and almost castle-like, Capernwray opened my eyes and heart to our Creator even further as I learned about Him daily and traveled around Europe with my new friends whose passports showed they were from everywhere across the globe.

One of my closest friends I met during my year away (we'll call him Anthony) understands, too, how even those of us who love Christ dearly are capable of things we'd never, ever expected we were. His dream in life was to work for NASA. And I think he would have; he's brilliant. Soon after returning to the US when Capernwray ended for the year, he went into the air force. And somewhere in there, a crack began to form. My dear friend is on death row now, having done unspeakable things, destroying any hope for a bright future for all individuals involved. Including his own.

The day after Ben proposed, we boarded a plane to Georgia

because I was subpoenaed as a character witness in Anthony's tri-
al. It's everything like it is in the movies, and nothing like it at all.
Because this time it was *my* friend there in that front chair, behind
the dark-stained oak desk. His blue eyes no longer clear but instead
clouded with grief and remorse and the knowing of how devastatingly at fault he was.

But thankfully, our mistakes do not define us. They are not who
we are. We can allow Christ to use them for something beautiful.
It's been over a decade since that day in court, and though I prayed
for him often, I wondered what Anthony's life was like now. A few
weeks ago, I was surprised to hear the voice of his new lawyer on the
other end of a call I received after dropping the kids off at school.
Anthony's new legal team was traveling to Denver to meet with me.
My heart pounded so fast that I had to steady myself by leaning
against Ben's old Bronco as I stepped out of my car parked beside it.

My thoughts were racing, until they weren't. Memories of my
dear friend sped through my mind and screeched to a halt as I remembered peering into those remorseful blue eyes. I began to weep.
Heart-, gut-, and soul-wrenching sobs right there in my driveway.

Since meeting with his kind lawyers, who genuinely seem to
care about him this time, I now know how he is doing behind those
barred doors. I know that for over eleven years, he was holed up in
solitary confinement. *Eleven years* without human interaction, except
for one hour a day when he was allowed to walk around outside. I
grieve the life that could have been, and the life that is.

And yet I know that our God is capable of bringing about great
transformation. If we do wrong, we will have consequences. Anthony
knows this—even my youngest child understands this fact. We have
all messed up in great and small ways. And not just us. Think of those
we learn about in the Scriptures: Moses was a murderer. Abraham
committed adultery. And King David did both. But God transformed them and He transforms us, realigning us with Himself the
moment we turn our hearts to Him.

It's true that my dear friend will spend the rest of his earthly existence in prison, but that doesn't dampen the fact that God can still use Anthony in big, *big* ways. If he's able to forgive himself and allow Christ to fill the cracks and holes that have pierced his heart, he could be used in the revival of so many lives also behind bars.

Like our heavenly Father, the Japanese understand there is beauty in the restoration of brokenness. *Kintsugi* is the Japanese art of repairing broken pottery. By infusing fractured and damaged sections with gold, silver, or platinum, it treats the breakage and repair as an exquisite element of its history. Rather than trying to hide the fragments with super glue, they don't disguise it, but instead make it stronger and more dazzling than it was before the damage had been done.

As for me, God has used my errors to see people with deeper love and further-reaching compassion. He has established an incredible marriage of two people who strive for the brilliance of snow.

> *The most beautiful people we have known are those*
> *who have known defeat, known suffering, known struggle,*
> *known loss, and have found their way out of the depths.*
> *These persons have an appreciation, a sensitivity,*
> *and an understanding of life that fills them with*
> *compassion, gentleness, and a deep, loving concern.*
> *Beautiful people do not just happen.*
> Elisabeth Kübler-Ross [21]

Allow the errors and struggles in your life to strengthen you. Allow Christ's love to surround you when you derail. Allow His exciting plan to shine through. Let your heart shimmer with Christ's *Kintsugi*.

Exciting doesn't mean easy. I've mentioned before that His callings don't typically translate to simple and painless.

What exciting *does* mean is astonishing, breathtaking, and compelling.

Don't be scared that He will send you to Africa, ask you to sign up for the PTA, form relationships with folks struggling with abuse, or whatever that "thing" is that fills you with panic or dread. God's passion for your life will become *your* passion for your life if you truly release it all to Him. And that's one of the ways you know it's of Him: when His vision and your passions align. He made each one of us with talents and gifts and capabilities. He did that for a reason. Sometimes it just takes a while to figure out what those reasons are.

As a child, I felt defeated because I didn't think I was good at anything. My heart ached thinking I didn't have a single thing I excelled at. I was okay at several things, but never felt I had a single gift. In school, it was all about academics, sports, and music.

I wasn't competitive, and I wasn't an athlete. I could sing, but was more the backup type than the real star of the show. The only two awards I ever received while growing up were a first-place ribbon in hula hooping (I know, impressive) and a certificate in class for "Most Creative Dresser" (I'm not sure that was completely a compliment—I think that's what they give to the girl who doesn't glow success on anything).

In high school I really struggled to get good grades. I had boyfriends through the years who were, let's say, a bit lacking on the whole words of affirmation thing, and since that's one of my primary love languages, I took what they had to say (and didn't say) to heart. It wasn't until college that I realized I actually *was* smart, and even though I had to work a lot harder than some, it was possible to get onto the dean's list. And so I did.

It wasn't until my adult years that I came to see what my God-given gifts are and how He wants to use them. It's sad, really, that it's taken this many years to open my eyes to so many things I was born to love. I stuffed them away, thinking because they didn't have anything to do with academics, sports, or music, they weren't worthwhile at all.

But now I see that the "Most Creative Dresser" award was a

precursor to my love of creating in general. I love fashion, interior design, and making things pretty. There's nothing wrong with pretty, and with it, I have realized the gift of hospitality had been given to me. Through the years God has used my passion to embolden women in ways that it's become almost a ministry. Building them up, making them feel beautiful both inside and out. He has helped create a home that is inviting for both my family and for others. He has brought opportunity upon opportunity to be used in blessing other women by helping them make their spaces filled with their personalities and beauty as well.

My love of fashion, cooking, graphic design, Jesus, families, women, and words has fused together into a blog, a mission field, and a lifestyle.

Had I not given my story to God on that particular day as I sat overlooking the Space Needle, I doubt I'd be so fulfilled. I wouldn't know my best story is the one *He* writes. Oh, what I would have missed! The children who wouldn't be mine! The husband who loves me so well would likely not be by my side! This book would be blank, and I never would have understood the real reason of my being on this earth.

> Your gifts will not be wasted. Your loves and passions will be established and encouraged.

Your gifts will not be wasted. Your loves and passions will be established and encouraged.

Adoption may never be part of your story. Africa may seem as far away as it does today. That's our story. Yours is special and unique and perfect for you.

Allow yourself to be interrupted by Christ. Because there's such beauty in it.

I used to think you had to be special for God to use you,
but now I know you simply need to say yes.
Bob Goff[22]

For Reflection

.... 🦢 ....

I hope that reading this book brought you hope, gave you strength, and cultivated a desire to live in the full glory of God's wonderful adventures He has written for your life. I wanted to be vulnerable in my story in hopes of inspiring you to know that you don't have to live one more day feeling out of control or uncertain of the future. I hope His love for you shines through each page and you can give all control over to Him. I don't want you to walk away after reading this book without being able to dig deeper into your own life, reflect on how you see God working, and further study God's Word in your favorite translation so that you can apply His truths to your life. I created this reflection section so that you, too, can find your life being beautifully interrupted by God.

Reflect on these questions, turn back to each chapter, and be inspired to write out your answers and thoughts in your own journal. Or grab the closest piece of paper and scribble away. Even write in the margins of this book. Pause between each question, think on your answer, or start a prayer as you let God mold your heart, mind, and spirit to think of His glorious adventure for your life.

CHAPTER 1
. . . .

REFLECT

I didn't realize that when I turned my back to adventure, I had unintentionally turned my face toward a safe and ordinary life. The thing is, God didn't create us to live unmoved and indifferent lives. He is a bold God who desires that we live audacious and courageous lives for Him.

REREAD: Psalm 85:10–13

WORK IT OUT

Reread C. S. Lewis's quote about being a living house on pages 13–14. Ponder and pray through the point C. S. Lewis is making. Could God be asking you to give Him the keys to your simple "house" so He can build a palace in its place?

Have you been living a little too safely like I did? Have you crafted a life for yourself that is so cautious and conventional that you're missing what God has actually created you for?

Share some occasions when you've said yes to His promptings, though you may have been placed outside your comfort zone. What happened as a result (either in your own growth or someone else's who was touched because you stepped into Christ's calling)?

Do you trust God enough with your life to consider anything He'll ask of you will be for great benefit? If the thought of trusting Him that much leaves your stomach in knots, stop and write a prayer in your journal. Just write, don't overthink it. God can handle our worry, our uneasiness, and even our anger. He welcomes our authenticity so He can have a true relationship with us.

CHAPTER 2

· · · · · · · · · · · ·

REFLECT

After the Lord gave me a glimpse of His plan, I took control and went running with it. It took me awhile to realize that instead of taking control of what He was trying to share with me, I was to wait for more of the bigger picture. I'm reminded of those old Polaroid photos I loved when I was a kid. The moment the image began to form on the photo paper in my hand, I'd wave it around, expecting to make it develop faster. The thing is, I put forth a whole bunch of energy doing something that wasn't needed. The photo would become clear when it was time for it to.

REREAD: Job 22:21–23 and 1 Chronicles 22

WORK IT OUT

How have you gone ahead of God's plan for your life? Have you received a glimpse of your assignment or passion and run off ahead of Him?

Pray the Lord will reveal how walking *with* Him, rather than ahead of Him, ultimately gets us to our destination faster.

Are you willing to turn around and head back to God Almighty so He can build what He's designed you to be part of? I know you won't regret it!

CHAPTER 3

• • • • • • • • • • • •

REFLECT

After opening my hands and saying the words *Send me* to God, many of my tightly held worries dissipated because it was God who held them all, I no longer needed to. It wasn't an instantaneous shift in my life, but little by little, God began shifting my priorities and stretched my comfort zones. When I'm old and gray, I'd love to look back on the years behind me and feel as if I'd worked hard for the kingdom of God and that I made a difference in the lives of others so they, too, could know the love of God in a real and tangible way. I may not be able to change the whole world, but I can certainly be a pen in God's hands as He uses me in my own neighborhood and wherever else He deems a difference can be made.

REREAD: The Erma Bombeck quote used on page 25, Proverbs 19:21, and Exodus 14:14.

WORK IT OUT

Grab your journal and rewrite the Erma Bombeck quote in your own words. When you stand before God at the end of your life, what would you like Him to say about you?

How do we get our hearts positioned to give our story back to Him? How can we genuinely desire His plans over the ones we've created ourselves? I'm not going to lie, it's a slightly scary feeling to hand it over to Him to tend. Start a prayer to God about releasing control.

Let's concentrate on the concept of silence. Spend the rest of your day or even week without the normal noise of life. While most of us won't be able to literally step outside the busyness of our day-to-day and go to the mountains alone in hopes of spending time with the Lord, we can take steps to eliminate noise and distractions. Turn off the stereo while driving. Leave the television off as background noise. Go for a walk or run without your earbuds in. Be quiet and allow for stillness so you can hear God speak to your heart.

CHAPTER 4

• • • • • • • • • • • •

REFLECT

The Lord may have given you a glimpse of what His desire is for you. You may have heard a new kind of whisper in your heart, or maybe He shared what He *doesn't* want you to do, which is how He first spoke to me after giving my plans back to Him. God uses each season in our lives for His greater purpose. He used my season of waiting to prepare me for my next open door—working at a company that lead me to meeting my husband, Ben. I shared a few stories on thinking I was prepared for something, or knew how to do something, only to fail at it miserably. But as I look back on those failure moments, I learned that God will use us not because we have the ability, but that He will gives us the ability because He wants to use us.

REREAD: The story of David on page 51. You can also read more about this part of David's life story in 1 Samuel 16–18.

WORK IT OUT

If you are currently in a season of waiting for the next open door, how can you actively wait during this time of anticipation? Or if you've walked through that next open door, reflect on how you felt during your season of waiting. Journal out your thoughts and frustrations, and pen down ideas on how you can *actively wait*, rather than sitting on your hands and feeling discouraged by a meaningless-feeling season.

When have you jumped into something only to realize you weren't actually prepared to excel and thrive within it? Whether big or small, preparation is key in being successful.

Abraham waited twenty-five years from when he knew he would have a son to when Isaac was born. David waited over a decade from when he was anointed until he became king. In the New Testament, Saul, who later became Paul, also waited over a decade before going out on his first missionary journey. Why do you think God waited so many years between the calling and the fruition?

CHAPTER 5

· · · · · · · · · · · ·

REFLECT

I titled this chapter "Removing the Blinders" because God revealed a big part of my calling after attending a silent auction with Ben. Through a photograph of a boy from Malawi earnestly praying, God whispered the notion of adoption in my heart. However, sometimes when one wait is concluded as something is beginning to be realized, you enter right into another sort of season of wait. After learning and accepting this new information, God didn't reveal more than what was needed to get Ben and I moving outside our comfort zones. Our cross-country move and my new job working at a crisis pregnancy center were foundation stones in stepping into our calling.

REREAD: Ecclesiastes 3

WORK IT OUT

In what ways could you view your current life season as God orchestrating things without feeling dissatisfied by yet another period of seeming pause?

How could the Danish concept of *hygge* (hue-guh) change the way you see living in a period of wait?

"Claiming the story God was writing, not simply the one I thought I wanted, I realized growth and comfort do not comingle." What does this quote from this chapter mean to you when referring to your own life's story?

Pray specifically for patience and understanding while in a season of wait. Trusting God to write your story doesn't negate the fact that frustrations or impatience may creep into your thoughts because what He's asking you to do is outside your agenda or timeline—whether He's given you a big-feeling assignment or simply asked you to wait. Pray that God keeps your willingness to follow Him in the forefront of your mind.

CHAPTER 6

• • • • • • • • • • • •

REFLECT

I had a completely incorrect view of what life with children looked like, but I also had an inaccurate view of what life as a follower of Christ resembled: Christ died for *me*; God has blessed *me* with (fill in the blank); *I* am being used by Him. What I've realized is that the life I have is less about *me* and more about being a living example of what *God* can do. The Lord uses our unique experiences to embolden each of us to expand our dreams and glorify Him. Sometimes hard things come up in our life because He knows amazing strength, grit, or incredible circumstances will occur from it if we cling to Him.

REREAD: John 9:1–11, Ephesians 1:16–19, and Job 5:17–18

WORK IT OUT

In what way(s) have you gotten wrapped up in the me's and my's of your life, even in reference to what God is doing?

What expectations or false reality might God be asking you to give up so He can continue orchestrating a new story for your life?

What is going on in your life that you see as deep pain or obstruction to the story you feel you should be living? Could that pain or obstacle actually be placed within the pages of your life because God wants to show a watching world what He can do?

How would you explain the following quote to someone? "What do people mean when they say, 'I am not afraid of God because I know He is good'? Have they never been to a dentist?" (C. S. Lewis, *A Grief Observed*).

CHAPTER 7

· · · · · · · · · · · ·

REFLECT

Joy is something many talk about all the time. There are count-less cute little sayings on social media and hand-lettered prints on Pinterest. But when we're going through a rough season, these nice-ties seem trite and hard to actually grasp. It doesn't matter if we're living within the realm of Christ's calling or not; sometimes things are just plain painful and seeing the good in it is difficult. I'm not going to pretend having joy is easy all the time, but I refuse to stop fighting to hold on to it.

REREAD: Romans 15:13 and 2 Corinthians 11:23–27

WORK IT OUT

Is your joy dictated by circumstance? How would you rephrase this quote by Nirup Alphonse: "The joy we experience is a direct result of the perspective we have of Christ Jesus"?

Grab your journal and write out an honest prayer to the Lord as you consider Christ being the source of all hope and believe that He will infuse your life with an abundance of joy and peace in the midst of difficulty if you set your eyes on Him more than your circumstance.

Think through a life-altering experience and reflect on why it holds such a special place in your heart. Journal about how you see God's hand in that experience and how He used it to shape your story for His glory.

If reading this chapter reminded you of the depth and vastness of God's love for you, and how Jesus's sacrifice was the ultimate price for you to have eternal life, you can pray this redemptive prayer: *Lord, I need your help. I invite you into my life to be my Lord and Savior. I know you can fill the emptiness in my life, make me whole, and write the story for my life. Help me to trust You, and live my life to bring glory to You. Help me to understand Your grace, Your mercy, and Your peace. Thank You, Lord. Amen.*

CHAPTER 8

· · · · · · · · · · · ·

REFLECT

When we cannot see God's timeline, that is when faith steps in. This is what we saw in Hannah as we read about her in this chapter. She was an amazing woman who never gave up praying from the deep recesses of her heart. She wanted to be a mother more than anything in the world and clung to that hope and prayer for years and years . . . and years. As we moved forward with pursuing adoption and finally got a match with our daughter, we moved from one season of waiting to another. As the chapter is aptly titled, we felt like we were free-falling during the beginning stages of the adoption process, but ultimately, we knew God was waiting there to catch us.

REREAD: Jeremiah 29. You can also read the entirety of Hannah's story in the beginning chapters of 1 Samuel.

WORK IT OUT

Do you believe prayer can actually be a catalyst for change? What have you been praying about for a very long time? How often do you pray about it?

Grab your journal and talk with God about how you could thrive where you are at, whether that be during a time of wait or during a busy season, and listen as He continues to develop you and bring things into alignment with His plan for you in His kingdom.

Are you scared of freefalling, afraid of the unknown or failure? Pray about these fears, lay it all out before God, and listen as He whispers words of comfort—because He is there for us!

CHAPTER 9

· · · · · · · · · · · ·

REFLECT

I mentioned within the pages of this chapter that because I grew up in a Jesus-loving family, I've been praying since before I could tie my own shoes. That being said, prayer hasn't always felt comfortable. There have been times when I've felt my words to God fell flat and wondered if He heard me at all . . . and if He did, why didn't He respond the way I wanted Him to? I realize now that His unanswered prayers were actually a *no* or a *wait*, and I am so thankful many weren't answered in the way I thought they should be (If He had, I'd have no children and would be married to someone else!). Like anything, you just need to start. Prayer is simply having a conversation with God; it's putting words to what's going on in your heart.

REREAD: 1 Thessalonians 5:17 and reread the quote from Mother Teresa on page 122.

WORK IT OUT

How can you pray in an openhanded way so you recognize you want Him to redirect your prayers if you are asking something that is contrary to what He wants, and yet not simply using a blanketed and casual, "Your will be done"?

How can you stop saying the obligatory, "I'll pray for you" and show someone you actually believe prayer changes things and you actually care enough about them to petition the Lord on their behalf?

Have you felt a prompting to pray more yet you haven't really done anything about it? Why do you think you haven't? Are you intimidated? Do you think it doesn't actually change anything?

CHAPTER 10

• • • • • • • • • • • •

REFLECT

I was prompted by the Lord to dig into what contentment truly meant and what it signified in my story of my life He was writing. According to my thesaurus, synonyms of content are *comfortable*, *complacent*, *smug*, and the phrase *fat and happy*. I know I have craved the fat and happy side of life, but staying within my comfortable boundaries would mean I would miss out on so much God has in store for my life! Even if responding to God's call on your life means nothing will ever be the same, we must stir the embers and say yes. I also shared how I desperately prayed against serving in Africa—how scared I was of this unknown country. But little by little, God opened up my heart and now there are so many "I'd never" moments that have turned into "I cannot wait" ones.

REREAD: Philippians 4:11 and 1 Corinthians 12:12, 14–18

WORK IT OUT

Even those who follow Christ the closest can't honestly say they've never walked outside His will. How have you, perhaps even unintentionally, turned your face toward a comfortable life and gotten a little too content?

When was the last time you said yes to something out of your comfort zone? When you've gotten outside your comfort zone, what has happened? How have you grown during those moments?

One of the most beautiful aspects of doing life with others is learning we are each uniquely designed to bring glory to God's kingdom. Reflect on how you can use your unique gifts/talents to help your family, workplace, or community.

CHAPTER 11
· · · · · · · · · · ·

REFLECT

Because our friends and family didn't have the same calling that Ben and I did, they didn't agree with our decision and called us naïve. With loving hearts, they were attempting to steer us away from hard things. As doubt started to creep in and I second-guessed something God has laid upon my heart purely because someone close to me thought what He was asking was crazy or too big for little ol' me, I once again grasped joy, and leaned hard into building my trust in God. By urging the "safe" or the "easy," we are robbing others of the profound depth that can only come from clinging to Christ in affliction. Remember, this is your calling . . . not theirs. Who are you going to let run your life: well-meaning friends and family, or our heavenly Father Himself, who knows more than we could even begin to?

REREAD: Proverbs 3:5–6 and Ephesians 2:10

WORK IT OUT

When have you grown the most in character? During the simple times or during hard things?

There's something deeply textural about a woman who has experienced hard seasons. Her trust in God feels more solid and her joy more legitimate and well grounded. I want to be that sort of woman, even if it means taking an unpaved road with bumps here and there. After grabbing your journal, consider and write down characteristics you'd give a woman who has clung to Christ while walking through difficulty, frustration, and hardship.

Are you confident enough in what God is doing in your life to say yes to Him and no to others who may get upset at your dismissal? Reread the prayer on page 156.

CHAPTER 12

· · · · · · · · · · · ·

REFLECT

I've struggled with fear much of my life, seeing evil in my mind's eye as what-ifs surround my consciousness. Not so long ago, while running on a treadmill at the gym, I tuned my earbuds to the sounds of a news channel. In Russia, the nails of children were being ripped from their little fingers. Torture of the innocent. A bomber in the Middle East was reported to be a child. Local news of neglect, abuse. My eyes blurred and my heart raced. Stepping off the treadmill, I clutched my heart, unable to catch my breath—not from the push of running, but from an overwhelmed and angry heart, without the understanding of why life must be so cruel. I mentioned in this chapter that Ezekiel and I were locked up in fear, but faith was the key that let us out. I'll never begin to understand why He allows some things to happen and halts others, but what I can understand is all the goodness that still shines through.

REREAD: Matthew 6:34 and 1 John 4:18

WORK IT OUT

Do you struggle with fear? How do we keep from allowing fear from consuming us, blotting out any hope for joy and trust?

Can you hand your fear back over to God? Start a prayer to Him: *Here, take this. I'm fighting with this, Lord. Take it from my shoulders, it's too heavy.*

Satan finds ways to creep into our lives when we least expect it. Journal about times when Satan has tried to attack you. How can you actively combat Satan's attempts to get between you and God? Reread Psalm 91 for inspiration if you need it.

CHAPTER 13

• • • • • • • • • • • •

REFLECT

In chapter 11, we talked about saying yes to Christ even when everyone else thinks you should say no. You saw in this chapter that though God was asking Ben and me to do something crazy sounding (again!), He gave both of us the prompting. If you are married, know that if God is asking something of you, He will most certainly whisper the same calling upon the heart of your other half. The timing may be different, and one may have to wait until the other has the same prompting, but hold fast to the fact that if it's truly Christ's calling, both your hearts will be turned toward it.

REREAD: Romans 8:28 and Philippians 4:6

WORK IT OUT

Has God asked something of you that sounds crazy? Perhaps it's something so big that you can't imagine how it will possibly come to fruition because you feel so ill-prepared. But if you know the same bold God that I do, you'll recognize that though what He is asking seems impossible, He will make it possible. Not because you're capable, but because you're willing. What might He be asking of you during this season?

Do you like surprises? Not just surprise parties or an unexpected gift, but a life-altering, out-of-the-blue surprise. Journal about giving up control of your life, giving it over to God, and letting Him write your story (even one that might be full of surprises).

Does the passage about the widow and the oil in 2 Kings 4 change how you feel about God supplying all you need so His calling will reach fulfillment?

CHAPTER 14

• • • • • • • • • • • •

REFLECT

The words *Do not fear. I am allowing you to go through this for a reason* rolled through my mind every time I prayed in desperation when my child lied to our social worker and said I was abusive. Nothing I could humanly do would have taken me out of the situation I had been placed in and given a good outcome. All I had was God, and I knew I had to cling to Him.

REREAD: 1 Peter 3:13–18 and Matthew 5:10–12

WORK IT OUT

When have you felt such devastation over something that you didn't know if you'd ever be able to breathe freely again? Did you fall into lonely despair, thinking God had walked away from you, or did it force you to cling to Him tighter, praying He would help you see meaning in it?

Sometimes we suffer for doing good, as 1 Peter 3:17–18 and Matthew 5:10–12 speak about. Why should we welcome this type of suffering? Journal about how you can give over your fears, struggles, and sufferings to God and ask Him to help you endure and persevere through all situations—good and bad.

How can we endure well so when the world sees you struggle, they see Christ being glorified in spite of it?

CHAPTER 15

• • • • • • • • • • •

REFLECT

When life got crazy, I entered survival mode, and without realizing it, once again I accidentally left God behind. Realizing I was giving Him the leftovers of my life, He breathed the word *firstfruits* into my life and reminded me I needed to put Him first. Above everything. And Jesus loved me back to life. My season changed. Sometimes even good things put us over the edge in exhaustion.

REREAD: Isaiah 43:2, Matthew 11:28–30, and Deuteronomy 26:2

WORK IT OUT

What may He be asking of you in regard to giving firstfruits?

How can we remain in Him as we go about our day-to-day, saying our *yesses* and *nos*?

When was the last time you said yes to things before you asked God if you should jump in or not?

Reread the prayer of Jabez in 1 Chronicles 4. Pray that God enlarges your own borders and that complacency and fear won't hold you back.

I've realized people with struggles and suffering have a deeper understanding of God's love and grace. Sometimes it's exhausting, but it's been good for me. How could your struggles be good for you as well? What might He be teaching you through it? Read Psalm 119 and journal about how this psalm speaks to your current struggles.

CHAPTER 16

· · · · · · · · · · · ·

REFLECT

By now, you know I can be gripped by irrational fears. I shared my "you've been booed" story to illustrate a larger point about God's unwavering guidance and love in our lives. We only have to let Him in. I desperately want to be the type of person who trusts God enough, even through hard times, to see that His plan is worth it. Open the door, hand over the pen, give up the reigns—whatever cliché speaks to you—give your plans back over to Christ and allow Him to form a new thing within your life. Allow yourself to be beautifully interrupted.

REREAD: Deuteronomy 31:6–8 and Psalm 40:2

WORK IT OUT

John 6 tells us that life got intense for the disciples because they hitched their train to Jesus. Some were stretched beyond anything they wanted to endure so they decided it was too exhausting and walked away. We can judge these individuals all we want, and yet some of us are just like them. Living an exciting life doesn't mean it's easy. How can you keep finding the excitement in following God's plan for you, even during tough times?

Had you heard of the concept of *Kintsugi* before this chapter? How has Christ bound up your wounds and repaired the cracks in your life, making you even stronger than before?

You were placed on this earth for a reason and because you said *yes* to the Lord, you will undoubtedly make a difference in the world. Journal and pray about how God can use you. Listen to His whispers and promptings.

Acknowledgments

.... 🦢 ....

This part of the book has been the most difficult to write by far, because of the limited space and all the dear friends and family I want to recognize and thank. Even if your name isn't listed below, you know who you are and the impact you've made on me and this book. From the bottom of my heart—thank you.

God—thank You for urging me to the point where I realized Your plans for me would be better than anything I could have planned for myself. You're always prompting me out of my comfort zone . . . even right now my stomach is in knots knowing You're asking another thing of me and I'm having to release control again and give things over to You (again). I love You and pray You open hearts and minds to who You truly are through the pages of this book—it is solely for You and Your ultimate glory.

Benny—thank you for listening to Christ in all things. You inspire me to live with purpose and great love. Thank you for gently (not so gently) pressing me to write out our story. I never realized how much I love to write, and I owe that revelation largely to you. Thank you for hearing God's voice when sometimes my life is too loud to hear Him myself. Thank you for never giving up on me and loving me fiercely. And P.S. I think you're really cute.

Abreham, Ezekiel, Anton, Laith, Imani, and Elsabet—you are the most incredible individuals I've ever met. You know I'm not a crier and yet I'm forcing down tears as I pen down these words. Guys . . . God is *real*. He knows you, loves you deeply, and each of you were born for a very specific purpose. You were born and brought into our family for a reason, and God gave you one another for a reason. Each of your stories is important and God knows yours will help change the world for His glory. He has big plans for you! Some of you have known immense tragedy, but the Lord was with you through every second of it. You were never alone and will never be alone. We will always have one another and we will forever have Him.

Swanstrom and Anderson family—Mom and Dad, thank you for saying yes to the Lord's promptings. I always tell people I learned more from you two and the world you've shown me, than within the walls of school. Thank you for teaching me about adventure, even if I hated the word for the longest time. Erik, thank you for always being my friend and protector. The stories I share with my kids about how you love and value me inspires them to treat each other with love and respect. Thank you for being you, and for making the best decision ever in marrying Caroline. Little Sis, I couldn't love you more. The woman God has formed you into amazes me each and every day. Jane and Ben, thank you for your love. Thank you for allowing me to marry your son and thank you for pouring the most amazing support and love onto your grandchildren, even though we're far away. Sara, Mary, Chris, and Katie, I wish we lived closer.

Kiesha Marie Yokers—through the years and when I needed one the most, you have been such an incredible advocate and cheerleader for me. You make me laugh harder and think deeper. I am so blessed to call you my best friend. Thank you for believing in me when I haven't believed in myself. Through tears of grief or glee, I will sit with you always.

Unicorns (Kiesha, Meredith, Andrea, Amy)—thank you for your love, hilarity, and for believing in me. Our friendship is truly magical. Thick and thin, ladies.

Petra (AnneMarie, Tamara, Amy, Katie, Jamie, Jill) and the LIFEGATE ladies (Hannah, Crystal, Tatum, Abigail, and on…)— you are my Denver family. When doubt crept in while writing this book, you hit your knees and prayed your hearts out. You are my sisters and I adore you so.

Chad and Julie Cannon—thank you for seeing something in me that I didn't quite see in myself. Thank you for being a safe place and sounding board.

Nirup Alphonse—you believe in me like a parent believes in their child. As my pastor and dear friend, that is beyond humbling. Thank you for urging me along when fear rears its ugly head.

Jana Burson—the Lord couldn't have gifted me with a more wonderful agent than you. You are the perfect combination of friend and girl boss that I need.

Caleb Peavey—thank you for answering countless phone calls and responding to a million texts and e-mails as I seek advice and wisdom, of which you have much.

Leeanna Nelson and the entire Worthy team—I am truly humbled that you believed in me enough to put my words onto pages and into hands. The entire process has been a dream, thank you for being so incredible and supportive.

Moynihan family, Candee family, the other Anderson family, and Anil and Anna Idiculla—thank you for so generously offering your cabins for getaway weekends so I could write in solitude . . . and not be interrupted by my sweet family every five minutes. This book would not have been finished without those times away.

Notes

1. C. S. Lewis, *Mere Christianity* (New York: HarperCollins, 1996), 175–176.

2. William B.F Ryan and Charlotte Schreiber, "Red Sea," in *Encyclopædia Britannica Online* (Encyclopædia Britannica, Inc.), 2014, accessed February 7, 2018, https://www.britannica.com/place/Red-Sea.

3. "Conjugation of *Lacham*," *Pealim*, accessed February 7, 2018, https://www.pealim.com/dict/990-lilchom.

4. Bob Goff, *Love Does: Discover a Secretly Incredible Life in an Ordinary World* (Nashville: Thomas Nelson, 2012), 10.

5. Karen Karbo, *Gospel According to Coco Chanel: Life Lessons from the World's Most Elegant Woman* (Guilford: skirt!, 2009), 223.

6. Crystal Woodman Miller, "The Promise of Purpose," LifeGate Denver video, last modified October 29, 2017, http://www.lifegatedenver.com/watch-online/?sapurl=LyszMTI4L21lc3NhZ2VzL21pLytzZnh5Y3ZxP2JyYW5kaW5nPXRydWUmZW1iZWQ9dHJ1ZQ==.

7. Alex Beauchamp, "What Is Hygge?" *HyggeHouse*, accessed February 7, 2018, http://hyggehouse.com/hygge.

8. Wikipedia contributors, "Pearl," *Wikipedia, The Free Encyclopedia*, accessed February 7, 2018, https://en.wikipedia.org/w/index.php?title=Pearl&oldid=824350252.

9. Nirup Alphonse, "The Perspective and the Promise," LifeGate Church video, last modified December 10, 2017, http://www.lifegatedenver.com/watch-online/?sapurl=LyszMTI4L21lc3NhZ2VzL21pLytzZnh5Y3ZxP2JyYW5kaW5nPXRydWUmZW1iZWQ9dHJ1ZQ.

10. Beth Moore, "LifeWayWomen," *Instagram*, last modified Aug. 25, 2017, accessed Feb. 26, 2018, https://instagram.com/p/BYPhV1Xg0Gn/.

11. Ann Voskamp, *One Thousand Gifts: A Dare to Live Fully Right Where You Are* (Grand Rapids: Zondervan, 2011), 120.

12. *Roget's 21st Century Thesaurus, Third Edition*, "Content," accessed February 7, 2018, http://www.thesaurus.com/browse/content.

13. Martin Luther King Jr., *The Papers of Martin Luther King, Jr., Volume III: Birth of a New Age, December 1955–December 1956*, ed. Clayborne Carson (Los Angeles: University of California Press, 1997), 457.

14. *Roget's 21st Century Thesaurus, Third Edition*, "Withstand," accessed February 7, 2018, http://www.thesaurus.com/browse/withstand.

15. Henry Blackaby, Richard Blackaby, and Claude King, *Experiencing God: Knowing and Doing the Will of God* (Nashville: B&H Publishing Group, 2008), 236.

16. Max Lucado, *Fearless: Imagine Your Life Without Fear* (Nashville: Thomas Nelson, 2009), 6.

17. Ann Voskamp, *One Thousand Gifts* (Grand Rapids: Zondervan, 2012), 144.

18. Jill Briscoe, "IF:Gathering 2017—Jill Briscoe," IF:Gathering video, last modified February 5, 2017, https://www.youtube.com/watch?v=L3E7YD7xeNM&index=4&list=PLSc2QmGwTkQui0NQ7kcTJMKaqDYet5LTr&t=118s.

19. Tenth Avenue North, "Worn," *The Struggle*, 2012, compact disc.

20. Nirup Alphonse, "The Way of the Valley," LifeGate Church video, last modified August 6, 2017, http://www.lifegatedenver.com/watch-online/?sapurl=LyszMTI4L2xiL21p LytlemJhc3VrP2JyYW5kaW5nPXRydWUmZW1iZWQ9dHJ1ZQ.

21. Elisabeth Kübler-Ross, *Death: The Final Stage of Growth* (New York: Touchstone, 1974), 96.

22. Bob Goff, *Love Does: Discover a Secretly Incredible Life in an Ordinary World* (Nashville: Thomas Nelson, 2012), 59.

About the Author

.... 🦢 ....

TERESA SWANSTROM ANDERSON is living the life she thought she never wanted. With an art history degree and dreams of living in Europe as a curator, Teresa had big plans for herself. She had no desire to have kids—didn't even like them—but after a decision to lay her exciting plans at the feet of Christ, God began changing her heart little by little and while dating the man who eventually became her husband, the two felt called to adopt from Africa. Now, Teresa's house is bursting at the seams with the loves of her life—her husband, Ben, and their six children, four of whom were born in Ethiopia—Abreham (18), Ezekiel (13), Anton (11), Laith (9), Imani (7), and Elsabet (5). In her "spare" time, she speaks about motherhood, adoption, and following your passions, runs her popular blog (TeresaSwanstromAnderson.com), hosts gorgeous dinner parties, trains for half marathons, and infuses beauty into every corner of her Denver home. She believes in celebrating the every day, and instilling the love of God and others in her children's hearts. Through it all, Teresa grasps joy tightly amid the craziness of everyday life. She views her life as a series of redirected dreams, stumbling, falling, getting up, and wondering if she is investing her time where it matters most. To keep up with Teresa and her loud and silly family, head over to TeresaSwanstromAnderson.com.

WANT MORE OF WHAT YOU'VE READ HERE?

Head to TeresaSwanstromAnderson.com

My desire is to serve you and arrange a place
where we can sit and exhale for a few minutes.
I pray that you find this to be a place of nourishment
for an everyday, beautiful life.

Take Joy,
Teresa

WANT TO HEAR TERESA SPEAK TO YOUR GROUP?

Email Hello@teresaswanstromanderson.com
to book Teresa for your next event.

IF YOU ENJOYED THIS BOOK, WILL YOU CONSIDER SHARING THE MESSAGE WITH OTHERS?

Mention the book in a blog post or through Facebook, Twitter, Pinterest, or upload a picture through Instagram.

Recommend this book to those in your small group, book club, workplace, and classes.

Head over to facebook.com/TeresaSwanstromAnderson, "LIKE" the page, and post a comment as to what you enjoyed the most.

Post a picture of the book on Instagram with the caption: "I recommend reading #BeautifullyInterrupted by @teresaswanstromanderson // @worthypub"

Pick up a copy for someone you know who would be challenged and encouraged by this message.

Write a book review online.

Visit us at worthypublishing.com

twitter.com/worthypub

instagram.com/worthypub

facebook.com/worthypublishing

youtube.com/worthypublishing